Internet Activism

Other Books in the Current Controversies Series

Current
CONTROVERSIES

Internet Activism

Sylvia Engdahl, Book Editor

GREENHAVEN PRESS
A part of Gale, Cengage Learning

GALE
CENGAGE Learning·

Detroit • New York • San Francisco • New Haven, Conn • Waterville, Maine • London

Elizabeth Des Chenes, *Director, Publishing Solutions*

© 2013 Greenhaven Press, a part of Gale, Cengage Learning

Gale and Greenhaven Press are registered trademarks used herein under license.

For more information, contact:
Greenhaven Press
27500 Drake Rd.
Farmington Hills, MI 48331-3535
Or you can visit our Internet site at gale.cengage.com

For product information and technology assistance, contact us at

Gale Customer Support, 1-800-877-4253
For permission to use material from this text or product, submit all requests online at www.cengage.com/permissions

Further permissions questions can be emailed to permissionrequest@cengage.com

Articles in Greenhaven Press anthologies are often edited for length to meet page requirements. In addition, original titles of these works are changed to clearly present the main thesis and to explicitly indicate the author's opinion. Every effort is made to ensure that Greenhaven Press accurately reflects the original intent of the authors. Every effort has been made to trace the owners of copyrighted material.

Cover image copyright © auremar/ShutterStock.com.

LIBRARY OF CONGRESS CATALOGING-IN-PUBLICATION DATA

Internet activism / Sylvia Engdahl, book editor.
    p. cm. -- (Current controversies)
    Includes bibliographical references and index.
    ISBN 978-0-7377-6876-3 (hardcover) -- ISBN 978-0-7377-6877-0 (pbk.)
    1. Internet--Political aspects. 2. Political participation--Technological innovations. 3. Internet--Social aspects. 4. Information technology--Political aspects. I. Engdahl, Sylvia editor of compilation.
    HM851.I56959 2013
    302.23'1--dc23
                                                                2013004120

Printed in the United States of America
1 2 3 4 5 6 7 17 16 15 14 13

Table of Contents

When a large rental-car company rented an unsafe re-called vehicle that resulted in the death of two girls, consumer safety advocates sought a law to prohibit rental companies from renting or selling cars that have been recalled for safety reasons. An Internet petition overcame the company's opposition to the legislation. Online petitions have also led to the reversal of unpopular policies of companies and of governments.

Online comments about the 2011 revolution in Egypt gave the impression that it had been brought about by social networking on the Internet, though few of the people in Egypt had Internet access. Internet activism was not what caused Barack Obama's victory in the 2008 US presidential election, either. Such events occur because of the offline actions of individuals.

Chapter 2: What Are the Benefits and Problems of Internet Activism?

Dana Klisanin

Psychologists have been studying the behavior of people who use the Internet and other digital technologies to benefit other people, animals, the environment, and world peace—for example, by signing online petitions or supporting click-to-donate campaigns. The term "cyberheroes" applies to them, and society should recognize their contributions and the benefits of Internet activism, rather than focus solely on the negative aspects of Internet use.

Jonathan Glennie

Although some observers worry about the negative effects of globalization, there are many more positive aspects. The tremendous improvement in communication brought about by the Internet has made it easy for people all over the world to show they care about worthy causes. The Internet gives committed offline activists the ability to mobilize large numbers of supporters.

Monica Hesse

Although some Internet campaigns have been successful, others attract large numbers of casual supporters who merely click on causes that are trendy simply to make themselves feel or look good. There is a danger that by joining an Internet group, people will feel less inclined to take real-life action, especially in cases where their commitment to the group is only nominal.

Chapter 3: Should US Foreign Policy Foster Internet Activism Throughout the World?

In 2010, US Secretary of State Hillary Rodham Clinton gave a speech about the power of the Internet to advance democracy and the need for tools to circumvent politically motivated censorship. In it she announces that the US government will apply connection technologies to its diplomatic goals and will work to promote freedom of expression on the Internet everywhere in the world.

In an interview, the head of a Pakistani human rights organization tells how in 2008, during the dictatorship of Pervez Musharraf in Pakistan, social networks such as Facebook and Twitter were heavily used, and people expected this would go on; but the new government has cracked down on Internet use and has blocked many sites without asking for cooperation from their operators.

The government of India has recently demanded that hundreds of pages on Facebook, Google, and Twitter be removed or blocked because of political unrest involving fighting between ethnic groups, which has been instigated by cell phone texting. It asserts that the websites contained "hate-mongering" material, but news coverage of the unrest has also been blocked.

In Russia, political activists are using the Internet not only to gain support on social networks but to raise money for publications, political rallies, and demonstrations. Many people contribute via a Russian online payment system, or in cash at public terminals, because they are afraid to donate openly. Recently, seven million rubles from twenty thousand people were raised during a month.

Foreword

By definition, controversies are "discussions of questions in which opposing opinions clash" (*Webster's Twentieth Century Dictionary Unabridged*). Few would deny that controversies are a pervasive part of the human condition and exist on virtually every level of human enterprise. Controversies transpire between individuals and among groups, within nations and between nations. Controversies supply the grist necessary for progress by providing challenges and challengers to the status quo. They also create atmospheres where strife and warfare can flourish. A world without controversies would be a peaceful world; but it also would be, by and large, static and prosaic.

The Series' Purpose

The purpose of the Current Controversies series is to explore many of the social, political, and economic controversies dominating the national and international scenes today. Titles selected for inclusion in the series are highly focused and specific. For example, from the larger category of criminal justice, Current Controversies deals with specific topics such as police brutality, gun control, white collar crime, and others. The debates in Current Controversies also are presented in a useful, timeless fashion. Articles and book excerpts included in each title are selected if they contribute valuable, long-range ideas to the overall debate. And wherever possible, current information is enhanced with historical documents and other relevant materials. Thus, while individual titles are current in focus, every effort is made to ensure that they will not become quickly outdated. Books in the Current Controversies series will remain important resources for librarians, teachers, and students for many years.

In addition to keeping the titles focused and specific, great care is taken in the editorial format of each book in the series. Book introductions and chapter prefaces are offered to provide background material for readers. Chapters are organized around several key questions that are answered with diverse opinions representing all points on the political spectrum. Materials in each chapter include opinions in which authors clearly disagree as well as alternative opinions in which authors may agree on a broader issue but disagree on the possible solutions. In this way, the content of each volume in Current Controversies mirrors the mosaic of opinions encountered in society. Readers will quickly realize that there are many viable answers to these complex issues. By questioning each author's conclusions, students and casual readers can begin to develop the critical thinking skills so important to evaluating opinionated material.

Current Controversies is also ideal for controlled research. Each anthology in the series is composed of primary sources taken from a wide gamut of informational categories including periodicals, newspapers, books, US and foreign government documents, and the publications of private and public organizations. Readers will find factual support for reports, debates, and research papers covering all areas of important issues. In addition, an annotated table of contents, an index, a book and periodical bibliography, and a list of organizations to contact are included in each book to expedite further research.

Perhaps more than ever before in history, people are confronted with diverse and contradictory information. During the Persian Gulf War, for example, the public was not only treated to minute-to-minute coverage of the war, it was also inundated with critiques of the coverage and countless analyses of the factors motivating US involvement. Being able to sort through the plethora of opinions accompanying today's major issues, and to draw one's own conclusions, can be a complicated and frustrating struggle. It is the editors' hope that Current Controversies will help readers with this struggle.

Introduction

> *"The role of online activism is to increase public awareness of what is being done, or needs to be done, in the real world."*

Originally, the Internet was a place for acquiring information and communicating privately with colleagues and friends. But as interactive web applications and social sites—sometimes called Web 2.0—began to proliferate, the prospect of their being used for political purposes drew considerable attention. Communications experts were excited by the possibilities. It was widely believed that the Internet would enable everyone to participate in democracy and that eventually the line between activists and bystanders would disappear.

Many users of social media do respond to political messages and appeals from worthy causes; sometimes thousands of them click on links to show their support, giving the outward impression that the public is far more engaged than was the case before interactive technology became available. But by no means do all of these users have any real interest in politics. If they agree with posted information about a cause, they click to show that they do and may even discuss it in a blog; but that does not mean that they are willing to take further action. The majority are apt to forget about the issue and move on to something else. Many observers find this upsetting. They have become disillusioned about the potential of the Internet to produce results, and now use the disparaging term "slacktivism" to refer to what they see as superficial activity that merely gives people an unwarranted feeling that they have accomplished something. Some worry that it will deter such people from doing anything of greater political importance.

Social media expert Evgeny Morozov wrote in *Foreign Policy* magazine, "'Slacktivism' is the ideal type of activism for a lazy generation: why bother with sit-ins and the risk of arrest, police brutality, or torture if one can be as loud campaigning in the virtual space? Given the media's fixation on all things digital—from blogging to social networking to Twitter—every click of your mouse is almost guaranteed to receive immediate media attention, as long as it's geared towards the noble causes. That media attention doesn't always translate into campaign effectiveness is only of secondary importance."

This view of Internet activism is widely held by commentators on social media, although there is no evidence that online activity leads to a decline in traditional activism. Furthermore, though many have said that it involves less risk than in-person demonstrations and therefore shows less serious commitment, this is true only in countries like the United States that permit freedom of speech. Journalist Jesse Lichtenstein, in the online magazine *Slate*, points out, "If hard-line regimes are watching what their citizens do online, then by reaching out to an online community, even the most passive 'slacktivist' is crossing a risk threshold and enrolling in a jointly risk-accepting community. The jailed bloggers of Egypt and Tunisia were well aware of this, and to me their blogging pales little in comparison with the courage of the Greensboro students who staged [civil rights] sit-ins."

In 2007, social media expert Ethan Zuckerman gave the first of several talks in which he introduced what has become known as the "cute cat" theory of digital activism. "I explained . . . that while Web 1.0 was invented so that theoretical physicists could publish research online," he wrote in a blog, "Web 2.0 was created so that people could publish cute photos of their cats. But this same cat dissemination technology has proved extremely helpful for activists, who've turned these tools to their own purposes."

In other words, large social websites were not designed to spread information about politics or worthy causes, in which most users are not especially interested. People are drawn to these sites because they enjoy sharing commonplace things in their daily lives, such as cat photos, which are popular throughout the world. But once at these sites, they see postings by activists. Moreover, it is nearly impossible for authoritarian governments to censor political postings without blocking the whole website; and in that case it is not only the activists who protest. The majority of citizens are apt to get angry at the government if it shuts down their favorite social site in order to suppress a few political statements.

For this reason, some experts say, it is not necessarily a bad thing if most of the people who visit a site are not seriously involved in activism when they click to show support for a cause. The larger the proportion of relatively unconcerned users, the less likely the site is to be censored. And at least some of those users may be influenced by the activist arguments they happen to see while there.

Another reason why some media analysts believe critics worry needlessly about slacktivism is that the perceived contrast between online political activity and offline activism often focuses on actions that are not comparable. Radio Free Europe journalist Luke Allnut, in his blog *The Tangled Web*, points out that it is misleading to compare traditional political activism, such as lunch-counter protests or anti-war demonstrations, with "some kid turning his avatar green." It would be more appropriate, he says, "to compare the kid with the avatar with the teenager 20 years ago who might have worn the button and signed the petition. . . . There was certainly ineffective activism—more about indicating preferences than achieving change—way before the Internet came along. I'm not sure many regimes have been brought down by street theater or effigy burning either."

A point on which everyone agrees is that Internet activism alone cannot produce major political changes. It is a supplement to traditional activism, not a replacement for it. No one has ever claimed that if a cause has many online supporters there is no need for offline activity. A political movement must be organized, with some person or managing group in charge, and as has been pointed out by many experts, networking is the opposite of hierarchal organization. The role of online activism is to increase public awareness of what is being done, or needs to be done, in the real world—and in some cases to raise funds, influence voters, or recruit people for offline participation. It can also facilitate the organization of offline campaigns by providing a means of communication between activists or, for example, by alerting people to show up at a planned demonstration. Merely counting nominal supporters, however, is largely symbolic. Thousands of clicks or tweets can make influential people notice a cause, and can bolster the morale of its advocates; but by themselves they accomplish little.

At present there is considerable controversy about the value and effectiveness of Internet activism. It is safe to say that it has been exaggerated by the news media, which have enthusiastically attributed demonstrations and even revolutions against dictatorial leaders to the influence of Twitter and Facebook. Yet Internet users are certainly better informed about what is going on in the world than people who do not have access. Whether that will have a significant impact on the course of events remains to be seen.

CHAPTER 1

Is Internet Activism an Effective Means of Political Action?

Overview: There Are Many Ways to Support Political Causes on the Internet

Learn the Net

Learn the Net is a privately-held company that develops electronic training products for consumers, businesses, and educational institutions.

When people hear the word "activism", what do they think of? For Africans, it may summon images of protests for independence and freedom. Many Japanese may associate the word with teaching Japanese youth that they have an important role in society. And for many U.S. citizens, evocative images of peace protests and equality movements from the 1950s to the 1970s arise.

While activism has taken many forms over the centuries, the information age has moved activism into a new phase. Spreading awareness of a particular cause once meant knocking on doors, writing letters, and calling people. Now people create websites, send e-mails, post messages to online forums, and use social networking tools to inform the masses.

This Internet activism (often referred to as e-activism) has fundamentally changed the way that we raise awareness and rally people to a cause. Now anyone with access to the Internet can participate in a growing number of ways, regardless of age and skill level. With this increased accessibility, campaigns of all kinds have seen significant increases in participation.

A powerful example of using simple technology to spread awareness of political unrest occurred after the Iranian presidential election in June, 2009, when protestors took to the streets after accusations of fraud.

Many turned to Twitter to relay information to the rest of the world.

Free Tools

E-activism takes many different forms and there are many small things you can do as an activist with the Internet as your tool. For instance, are you witnessing pollution in your community? You can shoot photos or a video with an inexpensive camera or even your smart phone, and then upload it to YouTube. You can also create a mailing list and spread the word to your neighbors. Here are some other simple things you can do to promote your cause online.

As mobile technologies continue to advance, integrating Internet applications into portable devices, e-activism can now be done on-the-go.

Blogging is an easy and productive way to voice your opinion and share information. Many activists use blogs as a tool in their arsenal. There are numerous sites on the Web that allow you to create a free blog. Some of the more popular include WordPress.com, Blogger.com, and LiveJournal.com. Most blogs include a technology called RSS that lets readers subscribe and receive new content when it's published.

Of course, posting blog posts doesn't guarantee readers. Social media tools like Facebook and Twitter can be useful in spreading the word about your blogging activities. Additionally, those same tools can easily be used as e-activist tools. Facebook pages are easy to join and make, and they typically draw in many people. An example of an activist Facebook page is Greenpeace International, garnering over 380,000 fans worldwide.

Twitter can also be used to spread information quickly using hashtags. A Twitter hash tag like "#savetheocean" may quickly unite thousands of people to sign a petition, donate funds, or attend a rally. This sort of "instant" feedback is valuable to those that organize activist events. Its "real time" nature also allows people to spread news of momentous political and social events, uniting people across Twitter's simple platform.

Online Community Groups

Another way to spread information is through the use of community groups. Sites like Yahoo! Groups and Google Groups makes it easy to create and run an online community group. Both sites allow you to organize a mailing list that can be sent to members of the group on a regular basis. The Freecycle non-profit movement hosts most of its community groups on Yahoo! Forums. The organization helps people keep their unwanted possessions out of dumps and landfill and in the hands of those who may need it.

A site like Care2, dedicated to activists, is another useful destination. Care2 promises to put "powerful tools" in your hand, making it easy to support the causes that mean the most to you. There are numerous causes like safe food and women's rights that can be supported using the site's many tools.

As mobile technologies continue to advance, integrating Internet applications into portable devices, e-activism can now be done on-the-go. This technology allows you to take to the streets while remaining connected to a steady flow of information. It also lets you share pertinent information with [others] on the spot. If you're explaining deforestation in South America to someone, you can easily provide statistics by using your mobile device. Sending SMS [short message service] messages to mobilize people for a political rally is another way to harness technology for a cause.

While e-activism has its critics, it isn't going to disappear. New causes and ways to spread awareness about them seem to appear on a daily basis. However, it's important to realize that technology is only one tool to accomplish a goal. Often it takes more than a few words on a blog or an e-mail to make a difference, but it's a positive start.

The 2012 Presidential Candidates Made Extensive Use of Internet Tools

Pew Research Center's Project for Excellence in Journalism

Pew Research Center's Project for Excellence in Journalism specializes in using empirical methods to evaluate and study the performance of the press, particularly content analysis. It is nonpartisan, nonideological, and nonpolitical.

If presidential campaigns are in part contests over which candidate masters changing communications technology, Barack Obama on the eve of the conventions holds a substantial lead over challenger Mitt Romney.

A new study of how the campaigns are using digital tools to talk directly with voters—bypassing the filter of traditional media—finds that the Obama campaign posted nearly four times as much content as the Romney campaign and was active on nearly twice as many platforms. Obama's digital content also engendered more response from the public—twice the number of shares, views and comments of his posts.

Just as John McCain's campaign did four years ago, Romney's campaign has taken steps over the summer to close the digital gap—and now with the announcement of the Romney-Ryan ticket made via the Romney campaign app may take more. The Obama campaign, in turn, has tried to adapt by recently redesigning its website.

These are among the findings of a detailed study of the websites of the two campaigns as well as their postings on

Facebook, Twitter and YouTube—and the public reaction to that content—conducted by the Pew Research Center's Project for Excellence in Journalism.

In theory, digital technology allows leaders to engage in a new level of "conversation" with voters, transforming campaigning into something more dynamic, more of a dialogue, than it was in the 20th century. For the most part, however, the presidential candidates are using their direct messaging mainly as a way to push their messages out. Citizen content was only minimally present on Romney's digital channels. The Obama campaign made more substantial use of citizen voices—but only in one area: the "news blog" on its website where that content could be completely controlled.

The gap was the greatest on Twitter, where the Romney campaign averaged just one tweet per day versus 29 for the Obama campaign.

Different Arguments Used

The study of the direct messaging of the candidates also reveals something about the arguments the two sides are using to win voters. Romney's campaign was twice as likely to talk about Obama (about a third of his content) as the president was to talk about his challenger (14% of his content). That began to change some in late July [2012] when the Obama campaign revamped its website.

And while the troubled economy was the No. 1 issue in both candidates' digital messaging, the two camps talk about that issue in distinctly different ways. Romney's discussion focuses on jobs. Obama's discussion of the economy is partly philosophical, a discourse on the importance of the middle class and competing visions for the future.

This is the fourth presidential election cycle in which the Project for Excellence in Journalism [PEJ] has analyzed digital campaign communications. This year, in addition to the campaign websites, PEJ broadened its analysis to include an in-depth examination of content posted on Facebook, Twitter and YouTube, areas that were either in their infancy or that candidates made no use of four years ago. The study encompassed an examination of the direct messaging from the campaigns for 14 days during the summer, from June 4 to June 17, 2012, a period in which the two campaigns together published a total of 782 posts. The study also included audits of the candidates' websites in June and again in late July.

The changes from 2008 go beyond the candidates adding social media channels. The Obama campaign has also localized its digital messaging significantly, adding state-by-state content pages filled with local information. It has also largely eliminated a role for the mainstream press. Four years ago the Obama campaign used press clips to validate his candidacy. The website no longer features a "news" section with recent media reports. Now the only news of the day comes directly from the Obama campaign itself. (In the recent redesign, the Obama campaign also highlighted its "Truth Team" section which includes its criticism of the Romney economic plan as well as their accounting of Obama's initiatives—also as determined by the Obama campaign.)

The Romney website, by contrast, contains a page dedicated to accounts about the candidate from the mainstream news media, albeit only those speaking positively of Romney or negatively of Obama.

The Study's Findings:

- Obama's campaign has made far more use of direct digital messaging than Romney's. Across platforms, the Obama campaign published 614 posts during the two weeks examined compared with 168 for Romney. The gap was the greatest on Twitter, where the Romney campaign averaged just one tweet per day versus 29 for the Obama campaign (17 per day on @BarackObama, the Twitter Account associated with his presidency, and 12 on @Obama2012, the one associated with his campaign). Obama also produced about twice as many blog posts on his website as did Romney and more than twice as many YouTube videos.

- The campaign is about the economy, but what that means differs depending on to whom one is listening. Roughly a quarter, 24%, of the content from the Romney campaign was about the economy versus 19% of Obama campaign posts. But Romney devoted nearly twice the attention as Obama to jobs. Obama's attention to the economy was almost equally divided between jobs and broader economic policy issues such as the need to invest in the middle class and how the election presents a choice between two economic visions. Another striking finding in the topics of the digital conversation is how much the agenda has changed in just four years. Gone from four years ago are web pages focused on veterans, agriculture, ethics, Iraq and technology. New are pages about tax policy—and the two campaigns overlap on fewer issues than Obama and McCain did.

- The economy may have dominated both candidates' digital messaging, but it was not what voters showed the most interest in. On average Obama's messages about the economy generated 361 shares or retweets per post. His posts about immigration, by comparison, generated more than four times that reaction; and his posts about women's and veterans' issues generated more than three times. This was also true of attention to Romney's messaging. His posts on health care and veterans averaged almost twice the response per post of his economic messages.

- Neither campaign made much use of the social aspect of social media. Rarely did either candidate reply to, comment on, or "retweet" something from a citizen—or anyone else outside the campaign. On Twitter, 3% of the 404 Obama campaign tweets studied during the June period were retweets of citizen posts. Romney's campaign produced just a single retweet during these two weeks—repeating something from his son Josh.

- Campaign websites remain the central hub of digital political messaging. Even if someone starts on a campaign's social network page, they often end up back on the main website—to donate money, to join a community, to volunteer or to read anything of length. A July [2012] redesign of the Obama page emphasized the centrality of the campaign website further. Rather than sending users to the campaign's YouTube channel, the video link now embeds the campaign videos directly into the website, where the only videos are the ones Obama wants you to see.

Obama's digital strategy targets specific voter groups—as it did four years ago—to a greater degree than Romney's.

Some may question whether younger voters were attracted to Obama because of his digital activity or whether Obama used digital platforms because it was a logical way to reach a natural voter base.

Visitors to Obama's website are offered opportunities to join 18 different constituency groups, among them African-Americans, women, LGBT, Latinos, veterans/military families or young Americans. If you click to join a group, you then begin to receive content targeted to that constituency. The Romney campaign offered no such groups in June. It has since added a Communities page that by early August featured nine groups.

How important is digital campaigning: does more digital activity really translate into more votes?

In 2004, Howard Dean used the web to generate early support and fundraising, but he failed to convert that into caucus or primary turnout. Barack Obama more successfully converted his use of the web in 2008 to stage an insurgent campaign and win younger voters.

But some may question whether younger voters were attracted to Obama because of his digital activity or whether Obama used digital platforms because it was a logical way to reach a natural voter base.

In 2012 ... voters are playing an increasingly large role in helping to communicate campaign messages, while the role of the traditional news media as an authority or validator has only lessened.

Changes from Past Campaigns

While there may be no simple answer, throughout modern campaign history successful candidates have tended to outpace their competitors in understanding changing communications. From Franklin Roosevelt's use of radio, to John F. Kennedy's embrace of television, to Ronald Reagan's recognition of the potential for arranging the look and feel of campaign events in the age of satellites and video tape, candidates quicker to grasp the power of new technology have used that to convey a sense that they represented a new generation of leadership more in touch with where the country was heading.

PEJ began studying the role of digital technology in presidential politics in 2000. In our first report, "ePolitics," candidate websites were yet to emerge; news websites and "web portals" were the gatekeepers of digital campaign information. PEJ that year studied 12 of the most popular sites and portals providing campaign news, a list that included Salon, the Washington Post and Netscape. The study found an emphasis on updating tidbits of information throughout the day, so much so that sometimes the most important event of the day—or week—never became headline news. On February 28, 2000, for instance, AOL never led with John McCain's speech in Virginia Beach attacking Pat Robertson and Jerry Falwell, even though it was not only the story of the day but a critical event of his campaign.

In 2004, PEJ re-examined the sites still in existence (and added two others); websites that year made a significant push toward offering users a chance to compare candidates on the issues—something almost entirely absent in 2000. News websites were also beginning to provide opportunities for users to manipulate and customize information; navigation, however, was often difficult. It was also the election cycle in which candidate Howard Dean transformed political campaigns by becoming the first candidate to use blogging, to use his website to organize "meetups," and to use other internet technology as a major part of his campaign.

By 2008, candidate websites were standard, and campaigns were clearly taking steps to try to control their message in ways that bypassed the traditional media. This was the year that Hillary Clinton announced her candidacy on her web page; and Barack Obama, albeit not entirely successfully, announced Joe Biden as his running mate on his website. Obama also used his site widely to invigorate a national grass roots campaign and built substantially on Dean's 2004 efforts to raise millions in small donations using the web. Our analysis also found that different candidates' campaigns differed widely in how well each had mastered technology.

In 2012, in short, voters are playing an increasingly large role in helping to communicate campaign messages, while the role of the traditional news media as an authority or validator has only lessened.

Internet Activism Via Online Petitions Can Bring About Change

A. Lambert

A. Lambert writes articles on Policymic, a website that describes itself as a democratic online news platform aimed at getting people engaged in debates about important issues in US politics.

A recent petition on Change.org about the nation's largest rental car company, Enterprise, has caused a stir among internet activists over the past couple of weeks and has demonstrated again that internet activism can lead to change.

A proposed amendment called The Raechel and Jacqueline Houck Safe Rental Car Act of 2011 was introduced to Congress last July by Senators Charles Schumer (D-NY) and Barbara Boxer (D-Calif.). The amendment would close a loophole that allows rental car companies to rent or sell recalled cars.

Despite widespread agreement on this legislation, last week Enterprise Holdings, which owns Enterprise Rent-A-Car, Alamo Rent A Car, and National Car Rental refused to support legislation and said that the company had already made "significant changes and improvements" in its inspection and repair practices of recalled vehicles and that proposed legislation is "unnecessary."

In 2004, two young women rented a PT Cruiser from Enterprise, not knowing that the car carried an unrepaired safety defect and was under recall. That defect caused the car to catch fire, killing both girls. In the ensuing court case, Enterprise admitted full liability and the settlement amounted to

$15 million in damages. But that case was a reminder that these and many other deaths could have been prevented through simple legislation.

There is already an existing law that prohibits manufacturers and new car dealers from *selling* recalled cars, but there is no law against rental companies renting or selling such cars. A study by the National Highway Traffic Safety Administration found that, on average, rental companies fix only about half their vehicles within 90 days from when the vehicles are recalled.

To solve the issue, Hertz Rent-A-Car and the safety-advocacy group, Consumers for Auto Reliability and Safety, reached an agreement to call for Congress to give the National Highway Traffic Safety Administration authority over rental car companies, not just car dealers and manufacturers.

Victories that have resulted from online petitioning are evidence that governments and companies sometimes do listen to calls for change when there is widespread support on the Internet.

A Successful Online Petition

The company's stubbornness to support this legislation was a perfect example of corporate interests impeding on the safety of its customers and all who share the road with them. But a recent online petition at Change.org last week has led to a change in Enterprise's position on legislation. Cally Houck, the mother of the deceased sisters, called for online activists to put pressure on Enterprise to support the proposed legislation. The petition went viral, and a day after it was posted on Change.org, the number of signatures grew from 1,500 to nearly 140,000. The internet response to Enterprise's position on safety through online petitioning was a clear signal to the company about customer concerns.

Just one day after the online release of the petition, Enterprise announced, "In the past, we believed that this step was unnecessary, but a growing number of people, including our customers and business partners, clearly want more assurance on this critical issue. . . . We hear them and what we've heard has caused us to rethink our stance." The company's support still falls short of endorsement of the proposed amendment by Senators Boxer and [Schumer], but it was a step in the right direction.

This is not the first cause that has gained traction and resulted in victories through online petitioning. Last fall, Bank of America rescinded its announcement about a $5 ATM fee as a result of an online petition. Not long after, Ecuadorian women who petitioned to close clinics that tortured lesbian patients posted a petition on Change.org that received 113,000 signatures, igniting protests in Quito and leading to an announcement by the government of Ecuador that it would close the clinics and launch investigations.

Online petitioning has been around for more than a decade, but the rise of online social networking has given this medium for activism a larger voice. Petitions are now much easier to circulate, and recent petitions have led to more victories than ever before. Even the White House has its own site specifically for petitions.

Victories that have resulted from online petitioning are evidence that governments and companies sometimes do listen to calls for change when there is widespread support on the internet, and that the internet is one of the best ways to garner support from all areas of the globe.

The Internet Campaign Urging Capture of Ugandan Rebel Leader Joseph Kony Is a Good Thing

Sonya Nigam

Sonya Nigam is the executive director of the Human Rights Research and Education Centre at the University of Ottawa.

My daughter stopped me before I went to work on March 7 and said, "Mom, you have to watch this!" It was a half-hour video produced by the American charity Invisible Children that she received from two friends via Facebook.

Wow, it is really something—an ingenious piece of video production that pulls at your emotions, draws you in, and makes you want to participate in the campaign to make Joseph Kony a household name. The video tells you about Kony, the leader of the Lord's Resistance Army that operated in Uganda and kidnapped children to serve in his rebel army: boys to kill and girls to serve as sex slaves. There is an interview of Jacob, a boy who was kidnapped but managed to escape. His brother was not so lucky. He was caught and killed by his captors who used a panga [machete] to cut his neck.

In one of the most moving scenes, Jacob says, "It is better when you kill us. And if possible, you can kill us, kill us. For us we don't want now to stay because . . . we are only two. No one is taking care of us. We are not going to school, so. . . ." When asked whether he would rather die than stay on earth, Jacob replies, "Yes. Even now. How are we going to stay in our future?" he asks. If his brother was still alive he would say to him, "I love you, but now I miss you, so it is better when we meet, we are not going to meet, but we may meet in heaven you see? So it is better I will not talk much. It will start something. Because if I saw my brother once again, I don't . . ." Jacob breaks down weeping like a small child.

Kony's actions are so evil the International Criminal Court put him at the top of its list of persons to be prosecuted for crimes against humanity—only he needs to be caught first. There was a prior campaign run by Invisible Children to put pressure on the U.S. government to provide support for the Ugandan army to find Kony and bring him in. President Barack Obama agreed to send 100 U.S. military personnel to help with this effort.

The KONY 2012 Campaign

However, because government programs can always be cut, the charity decided to begin a new campaign, "KONY 2012," to ensure that government support doesn't disappear. The idea goes if everyone knows about Kony, if he is made famous, then people will be more inclined to continue and add to the pressure on governments to bring Kony to justice.

This mobilization experiment is a game changer, when it comes to reaching youth.

This campaign encourages young people to buy an activism kit that includes posters, a T-shirt, and two bracelets. April 20 [2012], oddly the same day known by some as 420 or Cannabis Appreciation Day, is the day when participants will deploy and on April 21 people all over the U.S. and Canada will wake up to see lawn signs, posters, and T-shirts adorned with Kony's name. In conjunction, 20 celebrities, including [actors and singers] George Clooney, Justin Bieber, and Rihanna, have been recruited as "culture makers" to pass on the message about the campaign, and 12 leaders have been targeted as "policy makers," including our own Stephen Harper [the prime minister of Canada].

The interesting thing about this campaign is that because the video has gone viral—2.7 million viewers one day after the March 5 launch and almost 55 million by the morning of March 9—the campaign will show us if it is possible to create a bypass route to political power if the millions of people it has reached decide to mobilize.

The video itself does a pretty clear job in telling the viewer why this campaign will work. It uses a pyramid to describe how governments make decisions in the national economic interest as dictated by elites and then corporations controlled by elites market down to the masses. However, if the masses make enough noise, they can influence the government and bypass corporate and other interests. So, even if the U.S. or Canadian government has no national economic or security reason for being involved in Uganda, you and I can still make them do the right thing, just because it is the right thing.

Now in this case, I am not sure that it is the right thing, and I will get to that a bit later, but as an old-school activist who has stuffed many envelopes, organized workshops, and handed out buttons this mobilization experiment is a game changer, when it comes to reaching youth.

Criticism of the Campaign

There has been some pretty quick criticism of the Kony 2012 campaign. Because it is attracting primarily white people in the U.S., mostly girls and young women between the ages of 13 and 24, it recreates the same distorting power dynamics of rich versus poor and black versus white. Rather than empowering Africans, it empowers predominantly middle-class and upper-middle-class white kids, setting them up as saviours for disorganized black folk. Thus, the campaign ignores the recurring domination of North over South and just perpetuates it.

Even if Kony is found and tried, and there is a possibility that he may already be dead, prosecuting him will not bring peace to the region. The problems of violence in Africa are very complicated and this campaign is much too simplistic. Not enough of the money goes to the cause; instead it is going to the organization. Finally, there is the assumption that the help that the U.S. is providing to the Ugandan army is in the form of weapons.

The involvement of young women in international politics and global change is a thing to celebrate, not to denigrate.

Invisible Children has defended itself against these attacks in other *fora* [forums], so here I will focus on the criticisms relating to race, gender, and complexity.

While I find that the re-creation of colonial relationships is problematic, it is important to note that not all the middle-class youth involved will be white. There are a number of black people who are part of the middle class and are very active in projects connected to Africa.

The involvement of young women in international politics and global change is a thing to celebrate, not to denigrate. While the video pulls on emotional heartstrings to create empathy for the children who have suffered, I am not sure this is such a bad thing. There are many films and documentaries that seek to create the same emotional environment with a view to encourage people to act. Perhaps it is somewhat manipulative as a tactic, but it allows the viewer to remain engaged to hear the details of the story.

If young women respond to emotion more readily than men and are prepared to engage on the issue, then I say good for them. At the heart of every human being there is an emotional life that provides us with context and meaning. This is not something that we should pretend does not exist. For many young people, male, female, or trans, I imagine this campaign will be their first step into activism. The cost is only $30 and some time. This is a low-risk activity and for a few it will be a life-changing moment.

Internet campaigns carry the hope that our communities can organize to do the right thing, even when our politicians don't want to.

Activism Deals with Narrow Issues

Finally, regarding complexity, critics should remember that scholarship and technical solutions through national and international governmental bodies is the work area of professionals, not activists. You do not create social change through a course on political relations or international development. The video does not attempt to provide greater clarity about the sources and possible solutions to the wide variety of interconnected peace and security, health, and agricultural issues that Uganda and other African countries face, nor the role that our post-colonialism global economy continues to play in continuing the domination of the North over the South.

It deals with the very narrow issue of impunity for crimes against humanity. Although there may be disagreement over which level of perpetrator should be brought to justice, there is general agreement that Joseph Kony is a bad guy. Regarding the claim that the U.S. government will be spending money to arm the Ugandan army, which in turn will cause greater havoc, I doubt very much that American involvement will be without strict control. So let's start where we can agree and not imagine that one campaign can solve all the world's problems.

The Internet and ancillary communications products are the tools of younger generations of activists, as we saw in the Occupy Movement and also in the Arab Spring. Internet campaigns carry the hope that our communities can organize to do the right thing, even when our politicians don't want to. Whether or not one agrees with the Kony 2012 campaign, it will be interesting to see how it plays out, and you can be sure that there will be others to follow.

The Internet Campaign Urging Capture of Ugandan Rebel Leader Joseph Kony May Do Harm

Ethan Zuckerman

Ethan Zuckerman is a researcher at the Berkman Center for Internet and Society at Harvard University and the cofounder of Global Voices, a global community of citizen media authors that promotes participatory media in developing nations.

This Monday, March 5th, the advocacy organization Invisible Children released a 30 minute video titled "Kony 2012". The goal of the video is to raise awareness of Joseph Kony, leader of the Lord's Resistance Army rebel group, a wanted war criminal, in the hopes of bringing him to justice.

By Thursday morning, March 8th, the video had been viewed more than 26 million times, and almost 12 million more times on Vimeo. (Needless to say, those numbers are now much higher.) It has opened up a fascinating and complicated discussion not just about the Lord's Resistance Army and instability in northern Uganda and bordering states, but on the nature of advocacy in a digital age.

My goal, in this (long) blogpost is to get a better understanding of how Invisible Children has harnessed social media to promote their cause, what the strengths and limits of that approach are, and what some unintended consequences of this campaign might be. For me, the Kony 2012 campaign is a story about simplification and framing. Whether you ultimately support Invisible Children's campaign—and I do not—

it's important to think through why it has been so successful in attracting attention online and the limits to the methods used by Invisible Children.

Who Is Joseph Kony, and Who Is Invisible Children?

Joseph Kony emerged in the mid-1980s as the leader of an organization, the Lord's Resistance Army, that positioned itself in opposition to Yoweri Museveni, who took control of Uganda in 1986 after leading rebellions against Idi Amin and Milton Obote, previous rulers of Uganda. Museveni, from southern Uganda, was opposed by several armed forces in the north of the country, including Kony's group, the Lord's Resistance Army [LRA]. Since the mid-1980s, northern Uganda has been a dangerous and unstable area, with civilians displaced from their homes into refugee camps, seeking safety from both rebel groups and the Ugandan military.

Kony and the LRA distinguished themselves from other rebel groups by their bizarre ideology and their violent and brutal tactics. The LRA has repeatedly kidnapped children, training boys as child soldiers and sexually abusing girls, who become porters and slaves. The fear of abduction by the LRA led to the phenomenon of the "night commute", where children left their villages and came to larger cities to sleep, where the risk of LRA abduction was lower.

The Ugandan government has been fighting against Kony since 1987. In 2005, the International Criminal Court issued arrest warrants for Kony and four LRA organizers. The United States considers the LRA a terrorist group, and has cooperated with the Ugandan government since at least 2008 in attempting to arrest Kony.

Invisible Children is a US-based advocacy organization founded in 2004 by filmmakers Bobby Bailey, Laren Poole and Jason Russell. Initially interested in the conflict in Darfur, the filmmakers traveled instead to northern Uganda and began documenting the night commute and the larger northern Ugandan conflict. The image of children commuting to safety became a signature for Invisible Children, and they began a campaign in 2006 called the Global Night Commute, which invited supporters to sleep outside in solidarity with children in Northern Uganda.

As a nonprofit, Invisible Children has been engaged in efforts on the ground in northern Uganda and in bordering nations to build radio networks, monitoring movements of the LRA combattants, and providing services to displaced children and families. They've also focused heavily on raising awareness of the LRA and conflicts in northern Uganda, and on influencing US government policy towards the LRA. In 2010, President Obama committed 100 military advisors to the Ugandan military, focused on capturing Kony—Invisible Children was likely influential in persuading the President to make this pledge.

The Kony 2012 campaign, launched with the widely viewed video, focuses on the idea that the key to bringing Joseph Kony to justice is to raise awareness of his crimes. Filmmaker and narrator Jason Russell posits, "99% of the planet doesn't know who Kony is. If they did, he would have been stopped years ago."

The Invisible Children approach focuses on American awareness and American intervention, not on local solutions to the conflicts in northern Uganda.

To raise awareness of Kony, Russell urges viewers of the video to contact 20 "culturemakers" and 12 policymakers who he believes can increase the visibility of the LRA and increase chances of Kony's arrest. More concretely, Russell wants to ensure that the 100 military advisors the Obama government has provided remain working with the Ugandan military to help capture and arrest Kony.

Criticism of the Kony 2012 Campaign

As the Kony 2012 campaign has gained attention, it's also encountered a wave of criticism. Tuesday evening, Grant Oyston, a 19-year old political science student at Acadia University in Nova Scotia published a Tumblr blog titled "Visible Children," which offered multiple critiques of the Invisible Children campaign. That site has attracted over a million views, tens of thousands of notes, and evidently buried Oyston in a wave of email responses.

The Visible Children tumblr points out that Invisible Children spends less than a third of the money they've raised on direct services in northern Uganda and bordering areas. The majority of their funding is focused on advocacy, filmmaking and fundraising. It also questions whether the strategy Invisible Children proposes—supporting the Ugandan military to seek Kony—is viable and points out that the Ugandan military has a poor human rights record in northern Uganda.

As a set of Kony-related hashtags trended on Twitter yesterday, some prominent African and Afrophile commentators pointed out that the Invisible Children campaign gives little or no agency to the Ugandans the organization wants to help. There are no Africans on the Invisible Children board of directors and few in the senior staff. And the Invisible Children approach focuses on American awareness and American intervention, not on local solutions to the conflicts in northern Uganda. . . .

Other criticisms have focused on more basic issues: Kony is no longer in Uganda, and it is no longer clear that the LRA represents a major threat to stability in the region. Reporting on an LRA attack in north-eastern Democratic Republic of Congo, a UN spokesman described the attack as "the last gasp of a dying organisation that's still trying to make a statement." The spokesman believes that the LRA is now reduced to about 200 fighters, as well as a band of women and children who feed and support the group. Rather than occupying villages, as the LRA did when they were stronger, they now primarily conduct 5-6 person raids on villages to steal food.

Invisible Children's Theory of Change . . . and the Problem with That Theory

I'd like to start an analysis of Invisible Children's techniques by giving Jason Russell and his colleagues the benefit of the doubt. I think they sincerely believe that Kony and the LRA must be brought to justice, and that their campaign is appropriate even though Kony's impact on the region is much smaller than it was five to ten years ago. While it's very easy to be cynical about their $30 action kit, I think they genuinely believe that the key to arresting Kony is raising awareness and pressuring the US government.

I think, however, that they are probably wrong.

A military assault—targeted to a satellite phone signal or some other method used to locate Kony—would likely result in the death of abducted children.

Kony and his followers have fled northern Uganda and sought shelter in parts of the world where there is little or no state control over territory: eastern Democratic Republic of Congo, eastern Central African Republic and southwestern Southern Sudan. The governments that nominally control these territories have little or no ability to protect their borders, and have proven themselves helpless when international agencies like the ICC have demanded their help in arresting Kony.

Finding Kony isn't a simple thing to do. The areas in which he and his forces operate are dense jungle with little infrastructure. The small size of the LRA is an additional complication—with a core group of a few hundred and raiding parties of a handful of individuals, satellite imagery isn't going to detect the group—that's why Invisible Children and others are trying to build networks that allow people affected by the LRA to report attacks, as those attacks are one of the few ways we might plausibly find the LRA.

Russell argues that the only entity that can find and arrest Kony is the Ugandan army. Given that the Ugandan army has been trying, off and on, since 1987 to find Kony, that seems like a troublesome strategy. Journalist Michael Wilkerson, who has reported on the LRA for many years, notes that the Ugandan army is poorly equipped, underfed, incompetent and deeply corrupt. Past efforts to crack down on Kony have failed due to poor planning, poor coordination and Kony's deeply honed skills at hiding in the jungle.

Complicating matters, Kony continues to rely on child soliders. That means that a military assault—targeted to a satellite phone signal or some other method used to locate Kony—would likely result in the death of abducted children. This scenario means that many northern Ugandans don't support military efforts to capture or kill Kony, but advocate for approaches that offer amnesty to the LRA in exchange for an end to violence and a return of kidnapped children.

Invisible Children have demonstrated that they can raise "awareness" through a slickly produced video and successful social media campaign. It is possible—perhaps likely—that this campaign will increase pressure on President Obama to maintain military advisors in Uganda. As Wilkerson points out in a recent post, there's no evidence the President had threatened to pull those advisors. And as Mark Kersten observes, it's likely that those advisors are likely in Uganda as a quid pro quo for Ugandan support for US military aims in Somalia. In other words, the action Invisible Children is asking for has been taken ... and, unfortunately, hasn't resulted in the capture of Kony.

The Problem with Oversimplification

The campaign Invisible Children is running is so compelling because it offers an extremely simple narrative: Kony is a uniquely bad actor, a horrific human being, whose capture will end suffering for the people of Northern Uganda. If each of us does our part, influences powerful people, the world's most powerful military force will take action and Kony will be captured.

Russell implicitly acknowledges the simplicity of the narrative with his filmmaking. Much of his short film features him explaining to his young son that Kony is a bad guy, and that dad's job is capturing the bad guy. We are asked to join the campaign against Kony literally by being spoken to as a five year old. It's not surprising that a five year old vision of a problem—a single bad guy, a single threat to eliminate—leads to an unworkable solution. Nor is it a surprise that this extremely simple narrative is compelling and easily disseminated. . . .

An unintended consequence of Invisible Children's campaign may be pushing the US closer to a leader we should be criticizing and shunning.

The Kony story resonates because it's the story of an identifiable individual doing bodily harm to children. It's a story with a simple solution, and it plays into existing narratives about the ungovernability of Africa, the power of US military and the need to bring hidden conflict to light.

Here's the problem—these simple narratives can cause damage. . . .

What are the unintended consequences of the Invisible Children narrative? The main one is increased support for Yoweri Museveni, the dictatorial and kleptocratic leader of Uganda. Museveni is now on his fourth presidential term, the result of an election seen as rigged by EU observers. Museveni has asserted such tight control over dissenting political opinions that his opponents have been forced to protest his rule through a subtle and indirect means—walking to work to protest the dismal state of Uganda's economy. Those protests have been violently suppressed.

The US government needs to pressure Museveni on multiple fronts. The Ugandan parliament, with support from Museveni's wife, has been pushing a bill to punish homosexuality with the death penalty. The Obama administration finds itself pressuring Museveni to support gay and lesbian rights and to stop cracking down on the opposition quite so brutally, while asking for cooperation in Somalia and against the LRA. An unintended consequence of Invisible Children's campaign may be pushing the US closer to a leader we should be criticizing and shunning.

Do our simplistic framings do more unintentional harm than intentional good?

Can We Advocate Without Oversimplifying?

I am aware that I am oversimplifying the situation in northern Uganda . . . and also aware that I haven't simplified it enough. It makes perfect sense that a campaign to create widespread awareness of conflict in northern Uganda would want to simplify this picture down to a narrative of good versus evil, and a call towards action. While I resent the emotionally manipulative video Invisible Children has produced, I admire the craft of it. They begin with a vision of a changing global world, where social media empowers individuals as never before. They craft a narrative around a passionate, driven advocate—Jason Russell—and show us the reasons for his advocacy—his friendship with a Ugandan victim of Kony. The video has a profound "story of self" that makes it possible for individuals to connect with and relate to. And Invisible Children constructs a narrative where we can help, and where we're shirking our responsibility as fellow human beings if we don't help.

The problem, of course, is that this narrative is too simple. The theory of change it advocates is unlikely to work, and it's unclear if the goal of eliminating Kony should still be a top priority in stabilizing and rebuilding northern Uganda. By offering support to Museveni, the campaign may end up strengthening a leader with a terrible track record.

A more complex narrative of northern Uganda would . . . be lots harder to share, much harder to get to "go viral".

I'm starting to wonder if this is a fundamental limit to attention-based advocacy. If we need simple narratives so people can amplify and spread them, are we forced to engage only with the simplest of problems? Or to propose only the simplest of solutions?

As someone who believes that the ability to create and share media is an important form of power, the Invisible Children story presents a difficult paradox. If we want people to pay attention to the issues we care about, do we need to oversimplify them? And if we do, do our simplistic framings do more unintentional harm than intentional good? Or is the wave of pushback against this campaign from Invisible Children evidence that we're learning to read and write complex narratives online, and that a college student with doubts about a campaign's value and validity can find an audience? Will Invisible Children's campaign continue unchanged, or will it engage with critics and design a more complex and nuanced response.

That's a story worth watching.

Twitter Does Not Cause Revolution, People Do

Harini Calamur

Harini Calamur is a broadcast media entrepreneur, filmmaker, columnist, and blogger. She is a native of Mumbai, India, and teaches the course "Media and Culture" at Sophia College there.

You need to have been stuck under a rock in Antarctica or living in the furthest reaches of China to have missed the popular protest in Egypt that led to the fall of a thirty-year-old dictatorship of President Hosni Mubarak.

The revolution didn't happen because one morning the people of Egypt woke up and said "Ah! Nice morning, we have nothing better to do, so let's get rid of our government".

Rather, the protests were the culmination of 30 years of repression, economic shackles, rampant corruption and above all—the inability of the bulk of Egyptian population to have or meet aspirations of a better tomorrow. It was a popular revolution and the government fell because it could no longer get people to obey it—and that included the Army that refused to fire on its people.

However, if you were on-line and read or 'heard' comments from those in the know—you would think that it was a Facebook or Twitter revolution (17% of Egyptians have internet access and that was severely blocked during the revolution) or a 'social media-inspired revolution'.

Ever since president Barack Obama won his election in the US, the power of the social media to garner support for a cause or elections has been talked about. What has been ignored is the sheer grassroots mechanism—individuals—who manned the campaign.

Dedicated workers—in various parts of the USA—who used social media as one of the tools to encourage voters to turn up and vote for their candidate on election day. These people didn't spam—rather they sent targeted e-mails to a mailing list of around 13 million voters (around 10% of the total voters), got around 3 million to donate and so on.

While these 10% might have been great and strong supporters for Obama, he would not have won if a substantial chunk of the remaining 90% who were not part of the social network didn't vote for him.

However, the hype was such that many believed that but for social networking Obama—who incidentally is a brilliant and tireless campaigner—would not have won. So much so, in the last general election the most visible part of the BJP's election campaign in India was its online 'LK Advani for Prime Minister campaign'.

There were internet groups, social media, web advertising and the rest of web marketing brought into play on this campaign. To no avail. If anything, the BJP fared worse than it did when it didn't use social media to campaign. On the other hand, the Congress, which, has an embarrassingly sad web presence, managed to win and do better despite the fact that it did not use the social media.

You meet people [online] from similar backgrounds, similar values, and you extrapolate this behaviour to the remaining population.

There is genuine problem when you start mistaking the tool for the outcome. Just because you have a screw driver at home, doesn't make you an electrician.

While the analogy might sound nonsensical—that is exactly how those active on social media are seeing its use in polity and society. Internet penetration in India was around 5% in the last general elections, and while it should have grown since then, it is nowhere near the reach of television (around 50%). This means that 95% of voters have no internet, and 50% have no television. Campaigns in India have to be fought the old-fashioned way—household by household, constituency by constituency.

Revolutions happen because the bulk of the population rises up against a government. Parties win because a large chunk of the population votes for a party. While social media is great fun, and an effective networking tool—over reliance can lead to a certain kind of complacency.

You meet people from similar backgrounds, similar values, and you extrapolate this behaviour to the remaining population. There is a great danger in mistaking the wood for the trees if you take this approach.

So the next time someone tells you that the power of social media is going to bring down governments, or bring in government, don't argue with the converted—just smile—because it isn't true.

Expecting social media to deliver revolution or governments is a bit like expecting Coke or Pepsi to sell via social media without getting their ground distribution in place.

CHAPTER 2

What Are the Benefits and Problems of Internet Activism?

Chapter Preface

Observers disagree not only about the effectiveness of Internet activism but about the motivation of the people who participate. Many have commented that the support given to worthy causes online is merely superficial and that participants deserve little credit for activity that requires no real effort on their part. In a blog published by the magazine *Psychology Today*, however, psychologist Dana Klisanin criticized this view. She wrote:

> Currently, Internet activism and various forms of digital altruism are referred to with the pejorative terms, "slacktivisim" and "slacktivist". These words suggest that people who support a cause by performing simple online actions are not truly engaged or devoted to making a change. These terms confuse "ease of action" with "importance of action," diminishing the latter and the individual with it. The term "slacktivist" is yet another example of the ways we are focusing on the negative aspects of technology at the expense of its positive aspects. Rather than celebrating engagement in the world, "slacktivist" undermines human motivation, belittling endeavors that depend upon Internet technology and mass participation . . . and the achievements made possible through it.

In her opinion and that of many others, visiting free "click to donate" sites (whose advertisers donate a small amount to the specified charity for each click) and signing online petitions is important both to the chosen causes and to the people who engage in such activities. "Valuing our voices and raising them in whatever way we can to improve the world is a noble pursuit," Klisanin says. She believes that paying attention to the needs of other people, animals, and the environment shows that a person is more caring and mature than those who ignore them, whether or not significant time and effort are devoted to activism about these issues.

On the other hand, some commentators fear that effortless support of causes simply makes people feel good and may keep them from bothering to do anything truly helpful. The vast majority of online supporters, however, would never have taken a more active role anyway, just as most signers of offline petitions never become activists. Offline activism does not seem to have decreased since use of the Internet became common.

Of course, there are forms of Internet activism that are much more demanding than clicking, and in some countries, even dangerous. Though hacking is generally a destructive activity, "hactivism," when employed in the fight for justice under repressed regimes, can be a constructive one. However, whether a given instance of hacking for political purposes is legitimate activism or merely criminal behavior often depends on individuals' views of what constitutes injustice. In such cases, the desirability of being active rather than passive online is open to question.

Although in many respects the Internet makes it easier for those who choose to become politically active, it is by no means an unmixed blessing to activists, for it has also made government surveillance a great deal more efficient than it was before communications and expressions of opinion could be spied upon online. Some experts therefore feel that the disadvantages of Internet technology outweigh the advantages and that on the whole its influence on the fight against political oppression will be negative. And in fact, the attempt to make the Internet secure against surveillance may eliminate the very feature that originally offered the most promise—its ability to interconnect ordinary people all over the world. If that happens, the existing opportunities for activists to gain widespread support from less venturous citizens will be lost.

People Who Support Good Causes on the Internet Are Cyberheroes

Dana Klisanin

Dana Klisanin is a psychologist and the founder and executive director of Evolutionary Guidance Media Research & Design, Inc. She is also the executive director of the MindLAB at the Center for Conscious Creativity, a global nonprofit research and education organization.

Although the bulk of psychological research continues to focus on the negative uses of the Internet, i.e., cyberbullying and the cyberbully, the total number of people engaging in acts of digital altruism and other forms of pro-social digital activism exceeds 100 million. Who are these people? While there has been little investigation in this area, Klisanin theorized that the most dedicated among them represent the first incarnation of a new archetype: the cyberhero. Embodying a transpersonal sense of identity, as ideal forms, the cyberhero represents individuals motivated to act on behalf of other people, animals, and the environment using the Internet and digital technologies in the peaceful service of achieving humanity's highest ideals and aspirations, e.g., world peace, social justice, environmental protection, and planetary stewardship. . . .

[Psychiatrist] Carl Jung described "archetypes" as "collective patterns, . . . a typos [imprint], a definite grouping of archaic characters containing, in form as well as in meaning, mythological motifs." Jung explained these motifs as "appear-[ing] in pure form in fairytales, myths, legends, and folklore" and cited "the Hero, the Redeemer, the Dragon," as some of the most well-known. In 1938, the hero took on another form: the "superhero." [S.] Packer describes superheroes as "secularized forms of supernatural beings that populate folklore and legend and religious literature". As humanity blends moral action with digital technology, another variant of the hero, i.e., the cyberhero, is emerging. Interestingly, this merger enables certain characteristics of the superhero to find embodiment in the phenomenal world.

Positive psychologists are beginning to explore the character strengths and virtues associated with heroism, however we currently have few measures of this construct. Although understudied, heroism has been traditionally associated with courage, valor, and bravery: heroes are considered to be those individuals willing to risk their lives on behalf of others. Researchers examining the social construction of heroism have, however, identified additional elements of heroism including benefiting others and acting selflessly.

The Elements of Cyberheroism

Individuals using the Internet to act on behalf of other people are not risking their lives, however in some instances, websites that support digital altruism are designed such that the visitor confronts, not one, not two, not three, but a seemingly endless number of challenges in the form of "causes" that need urgent attention. From poverty to global warming to the threat of mass extinctions, these challenges are not easily solved, thus the individual seeking to bring them to an end, certainly faces some degree of psychological angst. Importantly, rather than turning away from these challenges, or pretending they do not exist, individuals who actively engage in digital altruism are confronting these challenges with the new tools that have become available to them.

To engage in this manner, the cyberhero archetype is embracing paradox. Traditionally, the hero is reactive, i.e., acting when the need to act arises. The cyberhero however, arising as it does from our globally interconnected "wired" world, is both reactive and proactive. It is "reactive" in that it reaches beyond physical boundaries to address existing problems (e.g., clicking-to-donate food), and it is "proactive" in trying to prevent the worst consequence of social inequality (i.e., starvation, disease, death) and environmental destruction (global warming, loss of habitat, extinction of species). The individual embodying the cyberhero archetype chooses to act all the while recognizing a certain futility in his or her singular act. To overcome this frustration, the cyberhero must posit individual action and collective action in simultaneity. The cyberhero knows he or she will not save the whales from extinction alone, but recognizes that we—an active community of like-minded individuals—may well succeed.

The cyberhero archetype provides an avenue through which a number of the superhero's characteristics are finding expression in the phenomenal world, albeit in a radically different form.

The cyberhero archetype appears to recognize global threats to social and ecological wellbeing as personal threats. Rather than requiring a personal confrontation with immediate danger, the cyberhero archetype requires a personal and collective psychological confrontation with current and/or impending species-wide dangers. Rather than setting out on an epic adventure to far away lands and encountering life-threatening dangers, as in the traditional heroic narrative, the cyberhero, paradoxically, both stays at home and sets off— into cyberspace with the goal of benefiting others. . . .

Because the Internet is the modus operandi of the cyberhero, s/he is able to imitate the dual persona, shape shifting, and speed of the superhero archetype. Dual persona and shape shifting are enabled through the use of an avatar, i.e., self-selected digital persona; and speed via the Internet's rapid transfer of data. When an individual uses the Internet, or a gamer sits down to play a video game, he selects a digital representation of himself, i.e., an "avatar". The individual is free to select his sexual identity, race, hair color, as well as a variety of other features; depending on the choices available he may choose to "shape-shift," identifying, for example, as a mythological creature or a Jedi knight. This ability to create a new identity for oneself, while in reality remaining the same person, mimics the dual-persona and shape-shifting characteristics of the superhero. Unlike the superhero, however, the cyberhero does not require an avatar in order to act on behalf of others, thus it cannot be said to inherit the psychic split posited of the superhero. Through embodying individual action in tandem with collective action, the cyberhero overcomes the split between communal and individual value systems.

While the hero archetype speaks to moral action, heroes are often associated with acting on behalf of a specific in-group (e.g., one's neighbors, community, or nation), the superhero, as originally conceived (e.g., Superman), embodies universal compassion and magnanimity (Packer, 2010). In using the Internet to act globally, on behalf of individuals of all religions, ethnicities, and nationalities, as well as animals and imperiled environments, the cyberhero appears to be embodying these ideal qualities. The cyberhero archetype provides an avenue through which a number of the superhero's characteristics are finding expression in the phenomenal world, albeit in a radically different form. In this regard, the archetype appears to be acting as a bridge, or conduit between the physical and imaginal worlds. . . .

The Significance of Cyberheroism

The human family is quickly approaching a point in time when global problems threaten to overwhelm social systems and psychological strength.

If history and psychotherapy provide any guidance to times of anxiety and threat, it might be in the observation that when people can contain their anxiety long enough to tolerate and actually face the dissolution of past certainties, they can often find the growing or emergent edge of insight and innovation. If, instead of denial or collapse, individuals and collectives can expand their awareness and allow themselves to clearly see what confronts them, they can rise to the occasion and become more than they were before. ([M.] O'Hara)

Today, we call for the survival of our ecosystem, and with it the preservation of a host of species, including our own. In response we have created a digital "caped-crusader."

The hero archetype has traditionally been associated with courage and fortitude, however [Z.] Franco and [P.] Zimbardo suggest that the hero archetype has been diluted in contemporary times, having become an adjective used to describe "inventors, athletes, actors, politicians, and scientist." They warn that by "diminishing the ideal of heroism, our society makes two mistakes . . . we dilute the important contribution of true heroes, [and] . . . we keep ourselves from confronting the older, more demanding forms of this ideal."

At first glance, the cyberhero might seem to add to such diminishment, i.e., rather than risking his life to help others, the cyberhero uses the technologies of cyberspace to actualize good deeds in the world, however upon closer examination we find that through extending the psyche to take on global challenges, the cyberhero archetype demonstrates expanded awareness, as well as psychological strength (having refused to permit the psyche to collapse under the weight of anxiety and threat). The archetype provides an innovative means through which individuals and collectives are using the tools at hand (e.g., smart phones and computers) to extend their humanity, becoming "more than they were before". Rather than diminishing the ideal of heroism, the cyberhero is poised to respond to an important need, that of "fostering heroic imagination" (Franco & Zimbardo.)

The cyberhero appears to be an emergent archetype arising from a transpersonal identification with the 'other' due to an enhanced understanding of interdependence that recognizes global threats to social well-being and planetary survival as significant consequences of non-action. Its emergence at this critical juncture in history, speaks to the superhero's manifestation at the beginning of World War II, which, from the Jungian perspective, symbolized humanity's joint psychological cry for power, strength, and immortality. Today, we call for the survival of our ecosystem, and with it the preservation of a host of species, including our own. In response we have created a digital "caped-crusader." The cyberhero archetype may be understood as a harbinger, an evolutionary guide of society. [B.] Banathy described "evolutionary guides" as entities (e.g., individuals, groups, corporations) that "giv[e] direction to the evolution of human systems and develop in those systems the organizational capacity and human capability to

1. nurture the physical, mental, emotional, and spiritual development and self-realization of individuals and the systems

2. extend the boundaries of the possibilities for freedom and justice, economic and social well-being, and political participation

3. increase cooperation and integration among societal systems and manage conflicts in a nonviolent manner

4. engage in the design of societal systems that can guide their own evolution by purposeful design

The cyberhero speaks to each of these mandates, and as such, this archetype may well serve a useful and important role as a guiding force in the continued evolution of humanity; indeed, the integration of compassionate action within digital technologies may well support the evolution of "homo curans," described as "compassionate man, man who cures"....

Results of the Cyberhero Survey

A total of 304 individuals responded to one or more of the questions [on a questionnaire], with 298 answering all questions. Of 302 individuals, 207 respondents were female, 90 male, and 5, transgender. Respondents were from 32 countries, with 69.7% from the United States. Of respondents, 301 reported engaging in one or more form of Internet activism considered beneficial to other people, animals, or the environment.

Results of Questions 6, 7, 8, 9, 10 support the premise that some individuals are motivated to act on behalf of other people, animals, and the environment using the Internet and digital technologies in the peaceful service of achieving humanity's highest ideals and aspirations, i.e., world peace, social justice, environmental protection and planetary stewardship.

Q6) Combined, 84.4% of respondents "agree" or "strongly agree" that through using the Internet to help others, they are contributing to conditions that promote peace in the world.

Q7) Combined, 74.0% of respondents either "agree" or "strongly agree" that through clicking-to-donate or signing on-line petitions, they feel a sense of unity with all the other people who engage in these activities.

Q8) Combined, 75.9% of respondents either "agree" or "strongly agree" that clicking-to-donate can have a significant impact on a cause, when a lot of people click each day. (This question was worded negatively, and is being reported positively).

Q9) Combined, 82.7% of respondents believe the Internet enables them to help others more than they could without it.

Q10) Combined, 85.4% of respondents either "agree" or "strongly agree" that they are being pro-active when they use the Internet to support the needs of other people, animals, or the environment.

Results of Questions 1, 2, 4, and 5, support the premise that respondent's (i.e., cyberheroes) have a transpersonal sense of identity.

Q1) Combined, 93.7% of respondents either "agree" or "strongly agree" that their life is interconnected with all the life forms on our planet.

Q2) Combined, 93.0% of respondents either "agree" or "strongly agree" that they enjoy acting on behalf of people in need regardless of their age, race, ethnicity, religion, or gender.

Q4) Combined, 86.4% of respondents either "agree" or "strongly agree" that they use the Internet to act on behalf of more than one "cause" or "charity".

Q5) Combined, 85.2% of respondents think the needs of other people are as important as their own needs. (This question was worded negatively, but is being reported as a positive value).

In summary, the data supports the stated premises. Some individuals are consciously choosing to use the Internet and digital technologies as a means to help other people, animals, and the environment. These individuals have a transpersonal sense of identity and view their on-line activity as contributing to conditions that promote peace in the world. . . .

The Importance of Studying Cyberheroism

The bulk of research and media attention has focused on the negative uses of the Internet, especially the activities of the cyberbully. This study demonstrates that there are also individuals using the Internet and digital technology for positive aims. While this statement may appear glaringly obvious, until now researchers have neglected to acknowledge or study this population. Through recognizing these individuals and their activities, as worthy of research and attention, we promote the positive side of human nature and the ethical use of the Internet.

Rather than placing all of our attention on cyberbullying, we need to begin giving equal attention to the opposite action: cyberheroing.

While the characteristics and traits of cyberheroes must be studied in a larger population, the archetype currently appears to embody a transpersonal sense of self. Importantly, 93.7% of respondents recognize their lives as interconnected with all the life forms on our planet, and 84.4% of respondents believe that through using the Internet to help others, they are contributing to conditions that promote peace in the world. If this recognition and pro-active stance holds true across the larger population of individuals who are actively using the Internet to help other people, animals, and the environment, (the "Causes" community alone currently has a membership of 150 million), it is not an exaggeration to infer that they hold great potential to address global challenges, especially when acting in concert. Social learning theory and research in social persuasion suggest that this pro-social behavior may increase as more individuals become aware of it and use social media to spread that awareness.

And awareness is spreading rapidly. Televisions with Internet-enabled capabilities now air programs with weblinks designed to support public health education and social networking sites, such as Causes already offer cause-marketing platforms through which users can elect to watch advertisements that result in donations to charity. Likewise, on-line games have been designed for the purpose of addressing social problems; some such as Zenga's Farmville have raised money for disaster relief through the sale of virtual game products, other's, such as Tim Kring's Conspiracy for Good, have used a combination of mobile and on-line gaming to build libraries in Zambia. More recently, the World Food Programme (WFP) and Konami Digital Entertainment have partnered to create Food Force, a game in which players fight hunger around the globe, i.e., the "money spent by players goes to fund WFP school meals projects in the real world". Games are evolving at a rapid pace and, as the above examples demonstrate, digital altruism has already become woven within them. As these initiatives expand, more individuals will have the opportunity to join the collective in addressing a myriad of challenges—in doing so they will be embodying the cyberhero archetype. Their actions will affect change in larger systems, for example changing economic structures through consumer mandated corporate social responsibility (e.g., requiring that donations be made to charitable organizations in exchange for viewing advertisements results in a larger percentage of revenue moving into the hands of non-profit organizations).

While this archetype requires further investigation, it is an important construct, for, in order to promote our higher natures, we must recognize and support acts of goodness, acts of compassion wherever we find them, including the Internet. Doing so means that rather than placing all of our attention on cyberbullying, we need to begin giving equal attention to the opposite action: cyberheroing.

[N.] Negroponte stated, "being digital" is "almost genetic in its nature, in that each generation will become more digital than the preceding one". In choosing to identify, study, and celebrate "cyberheroes" we provide a form through which individuals, especially the young, can recognize their ability to use Internet and mobile technologies to act compassionately on behalf of others. In summary, the cyberhero is a viable embodied archetype poised to expand the heroic imagination into the new millennium.

Internet Activism Allows People to Show They Care About World Problems

Jonathan Glennie

Jonathan Glennie is a research fellow in the Centre for Aid and Public Expenditure (CAPE) at the Overseas Development Institute (ODI). He writes a weekly blog at the British newspaper The Guardian *and is author of the book* The Trouble with Aid: Why Less Could Mean More for Africa.

There are many worrying trends in this modern era of globalisation, most notably the ease with which companies can operate and banks move money around, apparently outside any democratic parameters set by nations or an international community struggling to catch up with a rapidly liberalising context. But I have never been part of the "anti-globalisation" movement because there are so many positive aspects to globalisation.

The most important are those related to the incredible improvements in communication that the world has witnessed in the last two or three decades, largely due to the internet. If governments and the UN are failing to keep the excesses of private capital and corruption in check, these new global communities could be an important part of the answer.

Some in the UK would mark [British journalist] Michael Buerk's broadcast about the famine in Ethiopia as a turning point in their consciousness, but there are many other examples of when people in one part of the world realise that suffering and injustice thousands of miles away is of concern to them. Whereas once we cared only about the poor and homeless in our own villages, the world is now our village.

Nowhere is this more evident than in an internet campaigning phenomenon that in the space of four years has announced a new vision for what kind of world community is possible: Avaaz. Since my cousin forwarded me an email from the organisation about a year ago, I have clicked in support of campaigns ranging from banning cluster munitions, stopping a woman being stoned to death in Iran, protecting the oceans and, this week, calling on chocolate companies to boycott Ivory Coast until Laurent Gbagbo steps down. So I've been busy.

This is not about giving, it is about participating.

But not *that* busy. The beauty of Avaaz, of course, is how easy it is—you just click your support and within days 800,000 people are calling on the US and the EU to ban a pesticide they have probably never heard of, but that kills bees and thus endangers the ecosystem.

Internet Activism Supplements Traditional Activism

Some have criticised this kind of "clicktivism", claiming that it is a shallow form of protest compared with the interlocked arms of marchers of the famous campaigns of the last century. But it is not an either/or situation. All the campaigns Avaaz supports depend on deeply committed campaigners for their heart, evidence and credibility. But Avaaz gives me and its 6.5 million members worldwide a chance to say we care as well. Imagine how much more effective campaigns would have been in the past with this ability to mobilise national, regional or global pressure. Apartheid, Vietnam, women's rights.

Ecpat is a small British charity that fights the trafficking and abuse of children. Last year Avaaz decided to give a boost to Ecpat's pioneering work by focusing on the Hilton hotel chain's refusal to sign a basic code of conduct to train its staff to end possible abuse in its hotels. Rather than deliver the petition to the company headquarters, Avaaz announced that it would put up billboards in the home town of the CEO— boldly linking professional responsibility for a massive business with personal responsibility as a member of the human race. Risky, but it worked. One week and 310,000 signatures later, the Hilton group promised to sign (before the billboards went up).

Last year the Brazilian congress voted on a measure to bar politicians convicted of corruption from standing for office. Most thought the vote would fail, as so many of those in congress were themselves corrupt (estimated at 25%). But in the largest internet campaign in Brazilian history, 2 million people signed a petition supporting the legislation. It passed.

These and many other successes could make a real difference to millions of people. What is attractive about engaging in this way is that it combines surprising perspectives (not the same old gripes) with a stark understanding of the reality of politics. The common theme is reining in power—one of my favourites was a campaign against the Murdoch press taking more of a monopoly grip of British media. This is not about giving, it is about participating. While charity fatigue is a well-known phenomenon, I have yet to come across solidarity fatigue.

In an age of "accountability", some have suggested that the small team that runs Avaaz and send us its latest campaign obsessions are unaccountable. But the key to Avaaz's success is precisely its accountability model, one that some of the traditional NGOs [nongovernmental organizations] (who must be delighted and more than a little envious as they watch this phenomenon) might want to copy. Each potential campaign is trialled on a sample of a few thousand members before it goes live. If there is low take-up, it is dropped. Avaaz responds to its members as much as it informs and leads them.

One funky gimmick Avaaz has is allowing you to see the names of signatories who support a particular campaign. "Jane from Canada, Vikram from India, Colin from Wales". I have wasted plenty of time looking at these names as they roll in, strangers in another part of the planet demonstrating that they care about things I care about. In real time. In my mind, I think: "Nice one Jane, nice one Vikram." Like the neighbourhood watch group operating in my street, Avaaz makes you realise that there is a global community calling for justice and common sense in our globalising village.

Many People Click on Internet Causes Merely to Give a Good Impression of Themselves

Monica Hesse

Monica Hesse is a staff writer for The Washington Post.

Facebook activism, the trendy process by which we do good by clicking often, was in its full glory last week after the death of Iranian student Neda Agha Soltan, killed by gunfire in the streets of Tehran.

First, Neda showed up in our Twitter feeds, then in our Facebook status updates: "is Neda," we wrote after our own names. And when people started Facebook groups inspired by her death, we quickly joined them, feeling happy that we'd done something, that we'd contributed.

But whether our virtual virtuousness will result in real-world action is unpredictable, and has as much to do with human nature as it does with amassing enough numbers. This is the problem with activism born of social networking sites.

The numbers are impressive. News outlets cited the groups, with names like "Angel of Iran," as examples of public outcry, potential signs of a turning point in the disputed Iranian elections. The largest of these groups, called simply "Neda," currently has nearly 36,000 members; dozens more had 1,000, or 100, or 10.

Click click click. It was so simple to join.

And . . . now what? Are we done? Was clicking an end unto itself? Do our Facebook groups—which are today often treated as the official barometer for a cause's importance; more members *must* signify more gravitas—ever translate into significant change?

(And if not, what are we doing there?)

"I don't have a lot of time for rallies," says Charles Hilton, a Baltimore service technician. That's why he joined "Neda," founded by a Houston real estate agent named Ali Kohan. "I haven't been keeping up with the news a lot lately, but . . . from what I gather, there was no reason to target this woman." What Hilton knew of her story spoke to him. He was touched. So he clicked. It felt like a show of support his schedule could manage. He's not sure what happens now; he hasn't heard whether the Neda group has any actual activities planned, or what he would be able to participate in.

The Low Bar of Entry

Hilton illustrates what Mary Joyce calls "the pluses and minuses for the low bar of entry" of Facebook groups. Joyce is the co-founder of DigiActive.org, an organization that helps grass-roots activists figure out how to use digital technology to boost their impact.

The low bar of entry means that joining—or starting—a cause is easy, and that causes can reach and educate a wide range of people. That's the plus. But that ease also means that well-intentioned groups could balloon to thousands of members, most of whom lack activism experience.

It's harder to cite the failures than the successes, because there are simply so many of them, disintegrating before they reach the public's eye.

"Commitment levels are opaque," says Joyce, who last year took a leave from DigiActive to work as new-media operations manager for Barack Obama's campaign. "Maybe a maximum of 5 percent are going to take action, and maybe it's closer to

1 percent. . . . In most cases of Facebook groups, members do nothing. I haven't yet seen a case where the Facebook group has led to a sustained movement."

There have, of course, been big examples of single-event success: The Internet-based organization Burma Global Action Network began as one American's Facebook group, formed to support monks' protest. The group coordinated a global "day of action" in 2007 that drew protesters around the world. More measurably, the release of Fouad Mourtada, imprisoned for impersonating a member of Moroccan royalty online, was attributed in part to protests that began on Facebook and Flickr and spread offline. And politically, Obama's campaign was famously driven by social networking participation.

But more often the stories of Facebook activism look like Egypt's April 6 Youth Movement earlier this year [2009], in which a Facebook group calling for a national strike in support of laborers gained a much-publicized 75,000 Facebook members . . . and then fizzled out in real life.

In some ways, it's harder to cite the failures than the successes, because there are simply so many of them, disintegrating before they reach the public's eye. Even some of the success stories are qualified: Participation in the Burma network decreased as coverage of it fell out of the news, Joyce says.

Click-Through Activism

"Click-through activism" is the term used by Chris Csikszentmihályi, the co-director of MIT's Center for Future Civic Media to describe the participants who might excitedly flit into an online group and then flutter away to something else. In some ways, he says, the ease of the medium "reminds me of dispensations the Catholic Church used to give." Worst-case scenario: If people feel they are doing good just by joining something—or clicking on one of those *become a fan of Audi and the company will offset your carbon emissions* campaigns—

"to what extent are you removing just enough pressure that they're not going to carry on the spark" in real life?

A better scenario for Internet activism, Csikszentmihályi says, would be if causes could break down their needs into discrete tasks, and then farm those tasks out to qualified and willing individuals connected by the power of the Internet.

But plain old Facebook groups? Attention shifts quickly online. How many status updates that read "is Neda" last week read "is Farrah Fawcett" or "is Michael Jackson" just a few days later?

It's still too soon to tell what tangible change the thousands of virtual Neda supporters will effect. Some groups were founded as simply virtual memorials, with no plans for future action, and those groups have already fulfilled their duty. "Neda" is still drawing new members, though not as quickly as last week. Kohan, the founder, says that he hopes the group will turn into a foundation, and he's seeking donations from universities. Founders of other Neda groups, including the 4,000-member "Never Forget Neda," say they never expected their groups to grow so large, and are now considering how— and whether—to leverage the numbers further.

But what if we don't want to be leveraged? What if we just want to join?

A Fictitious Cause

Anders Colding-Jorgensen, a psychologist and lecturer on social media at the University of Copenhagen, earlier this year challenged his students to a competition for who could create the most-member-drawing Facebook group. Colding-Jorgensen personally founded "No to Demolition of Stork Fountain," a group asserting that it would oppose the transformation of the Copenhagen fountain into an H&M clothing store. Within a few days, 300 people had joined; by the end of the week he had 10,000 members. Not a bad effort for a group supporting *an entirely fictitious cause*. Stork Fountain was not, and had never been, in any danger of demolition.

Furthermore, anyone who bothered to visit the discussion forum would have seen that; in the forum Colding-Jorgensen had explained that the group was just a social experiment.

"But people just went in and joined," Colding-Jorgensen says. "They didn't read anything." The group continued to grow—at one point at the rate of two new members per minute—until it reached 27,000 and Colding-Jorgensen decided to end the experiment.

Are the [Neda] groups causes? Or are they accessories—a piece of virtual flair that members could collect to show off their cultural sensitivity, their political awareness?

What surprised Colding-Jorgensen about people's behavior on his site was that the group was "in no way useful for horizontal discussions." Users wanted not to educate themselves or figure out how to save the fountain, but to parade their own feelings of outrage around the cyber-public.

Or, as says Sherri Grasmuck, a sociology professor at Temple University who has studied Facebook profiles: "I become the social movement as an affirmation of my identity, rather than choosing the social movement because it matches my identity."

In the Neda groups on Facebook, many of the wall posts are actually links to people's individual YouTube videos, which discuss their anger at Neda's death, or links to other Neda Facebook groups so that visitors can join not just one group, but two or three or four.

Are the groups causes? Or are they accessories—a piece of virtual flair that members could collect to show off their cultural sensitivity, their political awareness?

"Just like we need stuff to furnish our homes to show who we are," says Colding-Jorgensen, "on Facebook we need cultural objects that put together a version of me that I would like to present to the public."

Last week, we wanted to take action in response to a horrible death. We wanted to show support to her family and to other innocent victims. We wanted to spread knowledge of a terrible incident. Did we mean for our clicking to go somewhere? Or were we presenting versions of ourselves?

These groups were all about Neda. But maybe they were also all about us.

Internet Activism Becomes Hacktivism When It Is Combined with Hacking

Jason Kong

Jason Kong is a student at the University of Pennsylvania and a staff writer for The Consul, *a publication of the university's International Affairs Association.*

You return to your computer after a long day's work, ready to check the heaven knows how many Facebook notifications you managed to garner after a week of Internet abstinence. You quickly type in your password—incorrect. Confused, you try again, no go. Bewildered, you check for caps lock and then give it another shot. Must have changed it without realizing, you think, as you go ahead and file a password recovery request. You head to your e-mail and sign in there, but again your try fails. As attempt after attempt is rejected, you begin to panic as you think of the possibility of someone else having access to your Facebook, reading through your e-mails, and having full access to all the information you put online.

As horrific as the above scenario might sound, it's only one of many nightmare scenarios lurking in wait for users of the Internet. With the Internet ingraining itself in just about every part of our lives, from connecting real-world relationships to setting up virtual stores to providing entertainment, the web has grown from its nascent form into an all-encompassing medium. The Internet's immeasurable stores of information and distribution mechanisms have made it a battlefield for groups vying for power. One needs only to look at recent examples of targeted attacks on key websites in the

South Ossetia War of 2008 and Israel's ability to subvert Syria's radar systems in 2007 air strikes to see the prevalence of cyberwarfare among disputing nations. However, nation states are not the only armed parties in the combat zone; computer hacker groups have emerged as a noteworthy contender in any battle over the World Wide Web. With growing threats to Internet and civilian safety, we must consider what limits, if any, should be placed on Internet expression.

At their core, computer hacker groups are a collection or community of hackers, those Internet users who detect and possibly exploit weaknesses in computers or websites. The history of these bodies dates back to the advent of the electronic computer in the 1980s. For the next thirty years, computer hacker's abilities have matched the increased sophistication of computer systems as initial hacking groups such as the Legion of Doom and Masters of Deception of the 1980's and '90s have given way to the high-profile groups of today such as Lulz Security.

The Hacktivism Movement

While the illegal breaking into of computers seems antagonistic and unfavourable, perhaps people would be more willing to grant sympathy to the surging "hacktivism" movement. As the name may suggest, hacktivism combines the practice of hacking with political activism, using entry into computer systems and Internet attacks as a means of expression and method of fueling change. Popular forms of hacktivism include altering web pages to produce political content undesired by the website's owner or denial-of-service attacks (DoS attack) where hackers slow down or make unavailable Internet services through overloading a site's servers. Less disruptive hacktivism tools include creating websites or software to achieve a political purpose. This can be seen in the case of the activist site WikiLeaks, and bloggers blogging anonymously about sensitive political issues.

Here, we see that it becomes difficult to distinguish hacktivism from Internet activism as a medium for political expression. Typically, internet activism consists of using electronic communication technologies to raise awareness about issues. For example this can be achieved through Facebook campaigns or chain e-mails. This can be contrasted with cyberterrorism, where the Internet is used as a medium for terrorist activities. One of the more prominent examples in recent history is the series of DoS attacks on Estonian government sites by a pro-Kremlin youth movement of Transnistria following the relocation of the Soviet World War II memorial "The Bronze Solider of Tallinn." Even the term cyberterrorism itself is incredibly nebulous, as there is no agreement among governing bodies what constitutes terrorist activities or how cyberterrorism should be defined.

One central theme of hacktivist groups that has become especially relevant is that of freedom of expression and Internet censorship.

With political speech being arguably the most important protection granted by the First Amendment and being recognized as a necessary universal human right, drawing the line between what is acceptable protest and what is not on the Internet is crucial. Making the task even more challenging is the Internet's transcendence of national borders. If any resolution achieved regarding protected speech on the Internet is not uniform or consensual, enforcement becomes difficult as extradition and international relations comes into play.

Recent Hacktivist Activity

It might be more helpful to ground a discussion regarding hacktivism in terms of recent events, especially with the increased amount of media attention given to hacktivist groups in the past year. Internet censorship and protected speech came to the forefront of the United States' attention when the whistle blowing site WikiLeaks began publishing diplomatic cables from the State Department in November of 2010. WikiLeaks provides a mechanism for news sources and whistle-blowers to share classified information that is then published and shared with large media outlets. Controversy arose as proponents of WikiLeaks praised its ability to provide transparency in government while critics denounced its actions as detrimental to national security and international diplomacy. The unintentional release of an unredacted version of the cables prompted further fears regarding safety for the lives of confidential informants. In the week following the U.S. cables leak, Amazon, PayPal, MasterCard and Visa Inc. all froze or suspended payments to WikiLeaks, which is primarily funded by online donations. Hacktivists responded by DoSing a number of websites in what was termed "Operation Avenge Assange." While similar Internet battles have been occurring for years, this instance brought the issue back into the nation's limelight.

From the WikiLeaks example, it is seen that hacktivism can represent a number of interests and political views, from transparency of government to human rights issues. One central theme of hacktivist groups that has become especially relevant is that of freedom of expression and Internet censorship. In 2003, a meme termed "Anonymous" began circulating around the Internet that held the idea of Internet users forming a digitized global brain. Since then, Anonymous has grown in membership and reputation as a collective of hackers or an identity that hackers adopt. Their secrecy, as their name might suggest, makes it hard to pinpoint any person or group as "Anonymous." Instead, members of Anonymous use Guy Fawkes masks popularized in "V for Vendetta" and an image of a suited figure with a question mark for a face to establish their identity.

In 2011, another of today's high-publicity hacker groups, LulzSec, was formed. The group's name is derived from the Internet acronym "LOLs" (laughing out loud) and "security." Since their formation, the group has been active in exploiting security flaws of highly public organizations. In June, 2011, LulzSec declared a partnership with Anonymous and began "Operation AntiSecurity," a series of hacking attacks. Targets included the United Kingdom's cyberterrorism branch, the Serious Organised Crime Agency, the Arizona Department of Public Safety, and the governments of Zimbabwe and Tunisia. Other government-targeted attacks by LulzSec include DoSing the Central Intelligence Agency's website www.cia.gov and releasing sensitive account information associated with the US Senate's www.senate.gov.

We as a nation or a collective of Internet users are at a crossroads regarding the appropriateness of hacktivism.

Hacktivism vs. Internet Censorship

Hacktivism has again been brought to attention regarding Internet censorship. The primary impetus to this past month's events in the United States were two pieces of legislation up for debate in Congress: the Stop Online Piracy Act (SOPA) in the House of Representatives and its Senate counterpart, the Protect IP Act (PIPA). These two bills sought to protect intellectual property and enforce copyright laws by increasing enforcement power of governing bodies and expanding the scope of forms of expression that fall under copyright legislation. As termed by one CNN reporter, the debate regarding the proposals soon became a battle of Hollywood versus Silicon Valley. As organizations such as the Recording Industry Association of America (RIAA) tried to push the bills through, tech giants such as Google and Facebook urged their users to voice their dissent. Opposition culminated on January 18th [2012] with Reddit, the English Wikipedia, and 7,000 other sites "blacked out" in a joint effort against the proposed legislation. This Internet activism was met with success as plans to draft the bills were postponed indefinitely. However, many free Internet advocates were disappointed the next day when they found Megaupload, a popular file-hosting site, was shut down and that several Megaupload executives had been arrested. In retaliation, Anonymous launched a series of attacks on sites including the Department of Justice, FBI, RIAA, and Motion Picture Association of America (MPAA). The attacks brought back down to earth the peaceful, white knight-esque efforts of the previous day's protests. Consequentially, Internet-interest groups have denounced these hacks as unproductive while legislators have pointed to it as a need for more regulation.

We as a nation or a collective of Internet users are at a crossroads regarding the appropriateness of hacktivism. As we weigh the pro's and con's of how much freedom of expression we wish to allow on the Internet, we have to remember that freedom is most at danger when safety is at stake. In the words of Benjamin Franklin, "he who gives up freedom for safety deserves neither." After seeing both sides of the issue, we must decide to either denounce these Internet hackers as irresponsible terrorists or herald them as champions of freedom.

If Internet Activism Is Forced to Go Underground, Democratic Communication May Be Lost

Alison Powell

Alison Powell is a fellow in the department of media and communications at the London School of Economics, where she researches digital media policy and open source culture.

The 'open' internet was supposed to give us a worldwide 'network society' where our communications would move from being controlled from above through broadcast models, and towards more horizontal 'mass-self-communication'. The excitement about the use of social media in the Arab Spring and even the furore over Anonymous' [a computer hacker group] (temporary) disruptions of some minor engines of capitalism suggest that we are still tantalized by the potential that technology appears to bring. At the same time, we become worried about exploits of the networked power of the internet—that come in the form of cybercrime and widespread breach of existing laws and norms like copyright.

Increasingly, the negative and disruptive aspects of the 'open' internet seem to be getting more attention than the potentially positive ones. Governments are concerned about the rise of cybercrime, the threat of filesharing to industries that depend on the control of intellectual property, and the control of dissenting speech. Along with industries and police, they strengthen intellectual property laws, prosecute and shut down file-sharing servers, track individual activists through social networks, and arrange with Internet Service Providers to block and filter problematic internet content.

So now we are in a situation where law, policy, and architecture combine to close down aspects of the 'open' internet. This has the paradoxical result of driving underground some of the practices that used to take place out in the open— beginning with some of the more unsavoury actions that happen on the internet, like file-sharing, but also extending to the kind of activism celebrated as an example of the democratic potential of the 'open' internet. On one hand the move away from the 'open' internet has inspired innovation in technologies like encryption, file-sharing and community wireless mesh networks, but on the other, it could have longstanding impacts on our communication environment.

Yesterday, the *Guardian* reported that Pirate Bay, in an effort to resist a High Court decision that file-sharing sites should be blocked, has moved to a new system for filesharing, using magnet links instead of displaying torrent files on its website. Magnet files are links with no files associated with them, which avoid tracking by containing very little information apart from an indication of the content they are associated with. The attraction of magnet links, according to SoftPedia, is that they make it easier for file-sharing sites to avoid accusations of wrong-doing in court. Other file-sharers use 'cyberlocker' technology where users pay for passwords to third-party file servers (often supported by advertising) where they can leave files they wish to share with others. Unlike torrents, cyberlockers (as well as magnet links) are difficult to monitor. They are also incredibly useful for benign purposes like sharing files between work and home, or collaborating with other people—the popular file storage system Dropbox is a form of cyberlocker.

These changes in practice are part of a move where some of the more unsavoury and disruptive products of the 'open' internet shift to dark corners where it is more difficult for governments and courts to get a clear picture of what is happening. They may respond by passing laws or enacting policies that attempt to address illegal behavior but in doing so may overreact to actions that are not illegal. For example, the UK's Serious Organized Crime Agency (SOCA) recently took over a music sharing domain after suspecting its operator of conspiracy to defraud—but not without initially posting a message implying that people who downloaded from the site may have conducted criminal offense. SOCA eventually changed the message, but the implication was that the use of *any* music site could be a criminal offence—which might well limit the number of people who want to use legitimate music-sharing sites, and push the less legitimate ones further underground.

As more of the unsavoury action goes underground, so might the kinds of communication we think of as 'open' and democratic.

Internet Activisim Is Going Underground

Activism too is moving into the dark shadows. One of the consequences of the Arab Spring has been a greater attention by governments to the communications of its citizens—and in parallel greater attention from activists to securing or encrypting their activities. The New America Foundation's Open Technology Initiative has been working on various prototype technologies meant to help activists avoid blocking, filtering, or internet outages. These include Commotion, a project that promises to use networked devices (mobile phones, laptops) as the points of connection in a mesh network that could grow to 'metro-scale'. Designed to be decentralized and to link devices together in ad-hoc formations when and where required, the project promises to create an alternative network as when needed. The *New York Times* reported on the project, which was supported by US government funds, calling it part of a 'stealth internet'. My old community wireless networking co-conspirator Sascha Meinrath is quoted as saying "we're going to build a separate infrastructure where the technology is impossible to shut down". The article also reports that other veterans of community wireless networking have moved away from creating networks that help to share internet access towards networks that are designed for secure communications—including the FunkFeur wireless networking project in Austria. This project has been building an autonomous network across the city of Vienna which is owned by its builders, a longstanding goal which, in case of threats or constraints on the commercial internet, could provide an alternative mode of communication.

Other projects go even further: ArsTechnica reports on The Darknet Project, another proposal for a worldwide meshed network, and Serval, a project to create ad-hoc wireless mesh networks using regular smartphones.

At one level, these projects feel like reinventions of the internet, which a collective burst of imagination framed as a platform for horizontal, networked communications. But now that the centralization and control of that platform is becoming evident, we need something else to imagine. The problem is that in creating darknets and super-encrypted dropboxes, all of the other benefits to speech that the internet has supported can get lost. One open internet, as compared to numerous separate and encrypted darknets, suggests the opportunity for global interconnection and communication. Already, social pressure and the habits of millions of internet users conspire to create 'echo chambers,' online. What remains is a shared imaginary of openness, of a resource to be governed by its users. The rise of super-encryption and darknets suggests that this imagined unitary resource is fracturing. As more of the unsavoury action goes underground, so might the kinds of communication we think of as 'open' and democratic. What do we risk when the activists go underground?

CHAPTER 3

Should US Foreign Policy Foster Internet Activism Throughout the World?

Chapter Preface

The growing use of Internet social media throughout the world was initially hailed by most experts as a means to weaken governments in totalitarian countries; they assumed that it would naturally lead to increased freedom in those countries. It seemed likely that through blogs, Facebook postings, and tweets their citizens would be able to arouse enough opposition to seriously challenge governments that had maintained power through banning books and controlling broadcast media.

After awhile, however, it became obvious that authoritarian governments are finding ways to censor the Internet, sometimes blocking entire sites. Moreover, they are often able to discover the identities of online political activists, whom they arrest. The United States—both officially and through private companies—has tried to help foreign activists, for example by providing technology intended to circumvent Internet censorship and surveillance. The US government has established a policy calling on all nations to support Internet freedom, outlined in a major speech given by Secretary of State Hillary Rodham Clinton in 2010. But increasingly, knowledgeable people have questioned whether this can work.

In 2011, Evgeny Morozov, a scholar who has studied this issue extensively, published a book titled *The Net Delusion: The Dark Side of Internet Freedom*. In it, he criticized what he called cyber-utopianism, the view that connection technologies are inherently democratic and that they generally favor citizens over oppressors. He pointed out the methods by which authoritarian governments can effectively combat Internet activism, as well as the fact that only a minority of citizens in totalitarian countries have Internet access, and that most of these people use it for entertainment rather than for any sort of meaningful political action. This book has been widely discussed by social media experts, and the majority now tend to agree with its arguments.

But there are still some who believe that the Internet will promote freedom and democracy. One of them is Clay Shirky, whose 2008 book *Here Comes Everybody: The Power of Organizing Without Organizations* was optimistic about its effect. Since then Shirky has pointed out cases in which Internet activism did work against foreign dictators, as well some where it failed. "As the communications landscape gets denser, more complex, and more participatory, the networked population is gaining greater access to information, more opportunities to engage in public speech, and an enhanced ability to undertake collective action," he wrote in 2011. "In the political arena . . . these increased freedoms can help loosely coordinated publics demand change."

Shirky has also pointed out that the prevalent use of media for non-political purposes is not unique to the Internet. "Far more people in the 1500s were reading erotic novels than Martin Luther's 'Ninety-five Theses,'" he wrote, "and far more people before the American Revolution were reading *Poor Richard's Almanack* than the work of the Committees of Correspondence. But those political works still had an enormous political effect."

Nevertheless, even if Internet activism does sometimes bring results, according to Morozov it also has the potential to do more harm than good because authoritative regimes quickly learn to use its tools for propaganda purposes and to identify dissidents, and also because people may be distracted from other forms of protest by the relative ease of supporting causes online. And in fact, it is not necessarily true that all Internet users want democracy—some of them may favor the governments they currently have.

Since publication of *The Net Delusion*, debate about the role of Internet freedom in foreign policy has focused on the contrasting positions of Morozov and Shirky. Both have presented important arguments, and it is too soon to tell which view will prove dominant.

Promoting Internet Freedom Throughout the World Is a Goal of the US Government

Hillary Rodham Clinton

Hillary Rodham Clinton was the secretary of state of the United States from 2009 to 2013. Previously, from 2001 to 2009, she was a US senator and from 1993 to 2001, during the Bill Clinton administration, was First Lady of the United States.

The spread of information networks is forming a new nervous system for our planet. When something happens in Haiti or Hunan, the rest of us learn about it in real time—from real people. And we can respond in real time as well. Americans eager to help in the aftermath of a disaster and the girl trapped in the supermarket are connected in ways that were not even imagined a year ago, even a generation ago. That same principle applies to almost all of humanity today. As we sit here, any of you—or maybe more likely, any of our children—can take out the tools that many carry every day and transmit this discussion to billions across the world.

Now, in many respects, information has never been so free. There are more ways to spread more ideas to more people than at any moment in history. And even in authoritarian countries, information networks are helping people discover new facts and making governments more accountable.

During his visit to China in November [2009], for example, President [Barack] Obama held a town hall meeting with an online component to highlight the importance of the internet. In response to a question that was sent in over the internet, he defended the right of people to freely access infor-

Hillary Rodham Clinton, "Remarks on Internet Freedom," US Department of State, January 21, 2010.

mation, and said that the more freely information flows, the stronger societies become. He spoke about how access to information helps citizens hold their own governments accountable, generates new ideas, encourages creativity and entrepreneurship. The United States belief in that ground truth is what brings me here today.

Because amid this unprecedented surge in connectivity, we must also recognize that these technologies are not an unmitigated blessing. These tools are also being exploited to undermine human progress and political rights. Just as steel can be used to build hospitals or machine guns, or nuclear power can either energize a city or destroy it, modern information networks and the technologies they support can be harnessed for good or for ill. The same networks that help organize movements for freedom also enable al-Qaida [terrorist organization] to spew hatred and incite violence against the innocent. And technologies with the potential to open up access to government and promote transparency can also be hijacked by governments to crush dissent and deny human rights. . . .

Some countries have erected electronic barriers that prevent their people from accessing portions of the world's networks. . . . With the spread of these restrictive practices, a new information curtain is descending across much of the world.

On their own, new technologies do not take sides in the struggle for freedom and progress, but the United States does. We stand for a single internet where all of humanity has equal access to knowledge and ideas. And we recognize that the world's information infrastructure will become what we and others make of it. Now, this challenge may be new, but our responsibility to help ensure the free exchange of ideas goes back to the birth of our republic. The words of the First Amendment to our Constitution are carved in 50 tons of Tennessee marble on the front of this building. And every generation of Americans has worked to protect the values etched in that stone. . . .

So as technology hurtles forward, we must think back to that legacy. We need to synchronize our technological progress with our principles. In accepting the Nobel Prize [in 2009], President Obama spoke about the need to build a world in which peace rests on the inherent rights and dignities of every individual. And in my speech on human rights at Georgetown [University] a few days later, I talked about how we must find ways to make human rights a reality. Today, we find an urgent need to protect these freedoms on the digital frontiers of the 21st century.

Internet Users Must Be Assured of Freedom

There are many other networks in the world. Some aid in the movement of people or resources, and some facilitate exchanges between individuals with the same work or interests. But the internet is a network that magnifies the power and potential of all others. And that's why we believe it's critical that its users are assured certain basic freedoms. Freedom of expression is first among them. This freedom is no longer defined solely by whether citizens can go into the town square and criticize their government without fear of retribution. Blogs, emails, social networks, and text messages have opened up new forums for exchanging ideas, and created new targets for censorship. . . .

Some countries have erected electronic barriers that prevent their people from accessing portions of the world's networks. They've expunged words, names, and phrases from search engine results. They have violated the privacy of citizens who engage in non-violent political speech. These actions contravene the Universal Declaration on Human Rights, which tells us that all people have the right "to seek, receive and impart information and ideas through any media and regardless of frontiers." With the spread of these restrictive practices, a new information curtain is descending across much of the world. And beyond this partition, viral videos and blog posts are becoming the samizdat [system under which Soviet dissidents circulated hand-copied texts] of our day.

As in the dictatorships of the past, governments are targeting independent thinkers who use these tools. In the demonstrations that followed Iran's presidential elections, grainy cell phone footage of a young woman's bloody murder provided a digital indictment of the government's brutality. We've seen reports that when Iranians living overseas posted online criticism of their nation's leaders, their family members in Iran were singled out for retribution. And despite an intense campaign of government intimidation, brave citizen journalists in Iran continue using technology to show the world and their fellow citizens what is happening inside their country. In speaking out on behalf of their own human rights, the Iranian people have inspired the world. And their courage is redefining how technology is used to spread truth and expose injustice. . . .

Just as terrorists have taken advantage of the openness of our societies to carry out their plots, violent extremists use the internet to radicalize and intimidate.

There are, of course, hundreds of millions of people living without the benefits of these technologies. In our world, as I've said many times, talent may be distributed universally, but opportunity is not. And we know from long experience that promoting social and economic development in countries where people lack access to knowledge, markets, capital, and opportunity can be frustrating and sometimes futile work. In this context, the internet can serve as a great equalizer. By providing people with access to knowledge and potential markets, networks can create opportunities where none exist. . . .

A connection to global information networks is like an on-ramp to modernity. In the early years of these technologies, many believed that they would divide the world between haves and have-nots. But that hasn't happened. There are 4 billion cell phones in use today. Many of them are in the hands of market vendors, rickshaw drivers, and others who've historically lacked access to education and opportunity. Information networks have become a great leveler, and we should use them together to help lift people out of poverty and give them a freedom from want.

The Internet Must Be Made Secure

Now, we have every reason to be hopeful about what people can accomplish when they leverage communication networks and connection technologies to achieve progress. But make no mistake—some are and will continue to use global information networks for darker purposes. Violent extremists, criminal cartels, sexual predators, and authoritarian governments all seek to exploit these global networks. Just as terrorists have taken advantage of the openness of our societies to carry out their plots, violent extremists use the internet to radicalize and intimidate. As we work to advance freedoms, we must also work against those who use communication networks as tools of disruption and fear.

The freedom to connect is like the freedom of assembly, only in cyberspace. It allows individuals to get online, come together, and hopefully cooperate.

Governments and citizens must have confidence that the networks at the core of their national security and economic prosperity are safe and resilient. Now this is about more than petty hackers who deface websites. Our ability to bank online, use electronic commerce, and safeguard billions of dollars in intellectual property are all at stake if we cannot rely on the security of our information networks. . . .

We have taken steps as a government, and as a [State] Department, to find diplomatic solutions to strengthen global cyber security. We have a lot of people in the State Department working on this. They've joined together, and we created two years ago an office to coordinate foreign policy in cyberspace. We've worked to address this challenge at the UN [United Nations] and in other multilateral forums and to put cyber security on the world's agenda. And President Obama has just appointed a new national cyberspace policy coordinator who will help us work even more closely to ensure that everyone's networks stay free, secure, and reliable.

States, terrorists, and those who would act as their proxies must know that the United States will protect our networks. Those who disrupt the free flow of information in our society or any other pose a threat to our economy, our government, and our civil society. Countries or individuals that engage in cyber attacks should face consequences and international condemnation. In an internet-connected world, an attack on one nation's networks can be an attack on all. And by reinforcing that message, we can create norms of behavior among states and encourage respect for the global networked commons.

The final freedom, one that was probably inherent in what both President [Franklin D. Roosevelt] and Mrs. [Eleanor] Roosevelt thought about and wrote about all those years ago, is one that flows from the four I've already mentioned: the freedom to connect—the idea that governments should not prevent people from connecting to the internet, to websites, or to each other. The freedom to connect is like the freedom of assembly, only in cyberspace. It allows individuals to get online, come together, and hopefully cooperate. Once you're on the internet, you don't need to be a tycoon or a rock star to have a huge impact on society.

The largest public response to the terrorist attacks in Mumbai [India] was launched by a 13-year-old boy. He used social networks to organize blood drives and a massive interfaith book of condolence. In Colombia, an unemployed engineer brought together more than 12 million people in 190 cities around the world to demonstrate against the FARC [Revolutionary Armed Forces of Colombia] terrorist movement. The protests were the largest antiterrorist demonstrations in history. And in the weeks that followed, the FARC saw more demobilizations and desertions than it had during a decade of military action. . . .

> *Both the American people and nations that censor the internet should understand that our government is committed to helping promote internet freedom.*

The United States Will Promote Global Internet Freedom

Now, the principles I've outlined today will guide our approach in addressing the issue of internet freedom and the use of these technologies. And I want to speak about how we apply them in practice. The United States is committed to devoting the diplomatic, economic, and technological resources necessary to advance these freedoms. We are a nation made up of immigrants from every country and every interest that spans the globe. Our foreign policy is premised on the idea that no country more than America stands to benefit when there is cooperation among peoples and states. And no country shoulders a heavier burden when conflict and misunderstanding drive nations apart. So we are well placed to seize the opportunities that come with interconnectivity. And as the birthplace for so many of these technologies, including the internet itself, we have a responsibility to see them used for good. To do that, we need to develop our capacity for what we call, at the State Department, 21st century statecraft.

Realigning our policies and our priorities will not be easy. But adjusting to new technology rarely is. When the telegraph was introduced, it was a source of great anxiety for many in the diplomatic community, where the prospect of receiving daily instructions from capitals was not entirely welcome. But just as our diplomats eventually mastered the telegraph, they are doing the same to harness the potential of these new tools as well.

And I'm proud that the State Department is already working in more than 40 countries to help individuals silenced by oppressive governments. We are making this issue a priority at the United Nations as well, and we're including internet freedom as a component in the first resolution we introduced after returning to the United Nations Human Rights Council.

We are also supporting the development of new tools that enable citizens to exercise their rights of free expression by circumventing politically motivated censorship. We are providing funds to groups around the world to make sure that those tools get to the people who need them in local languages, and with the training they need to access the internet safely. The United States has been assisting in these efforts for some time, with a focus on implementing these programs as efficiently and effectively as possible. Both the American people and nations that censor the internet should understand that our government is committed to helping promote internet freedom.

We want to put these tools in the hands of people who will use them to advance democracy and human rights, to fight climate change and epidemics, to build global support for President Obama's goal of a world without nuclear weapons, to encourage sustainable economic development that lifts the people at the bottom up.

That's why today I'm announcing that over the next year, we will work with partners in industry, academia, and nongovernmental organizations to establish a standing effort that will harness the power of connection technologies and apply them to our diplomatic goals. By relying on mobile phones, mapping applications, and other new tools, we can empower citizens and leverage our traditional diplomacy. We can address deficiencies in the current market for innovation. . . .

This issue isn't just about information freedom; it is about what kind of world we want and what kind of world we will inhabit.

There are companies, individuals, and institutions working on ideas and applications that could already advance our diplomatic and development objectives. And the State Department will be launching an innovation competition to give this work an immediate boost. We'll be asking Americans to send us their best ideas for applications and technologies that help break down language barriers, overcome illiteracy, connect people to the services and information they need. Microsoft, for example, has already developed a prototype for a digital doctor that could help provide medical care in isolated rural communities. We want to see more ideas like that. And we'll work with the winners of the competition and provide grants to help build their ideas to scale.

More Must Be Done to Ensure Worldwide Internet Access

Now, these new initiatives will supplement a great deal of important work we've already done over this past year. In the service of our diplomatic and diplomacy objectives, I assembled a talented and experienced team to lead our 21st century statecraft efforts. This team has traveled the world helping governments and groups leverage the benefits of connection technologies. They have stood up a Civil Society 2.0 Initiative to help grassroots organizations enter the digital age. They are putting in place a program in Mexico to help combat drug-related violence by allowing people to make untracked reports to reliable sources to avoid having retribution visited against them. They brought mobile banking to Afghanistan and are now pursuing the same effort in the Democratic Republic of the Congo. In Pakistan, they created the first-ever social mobile network, called Our Voice, that has already produced tens of millions of messages and connected young Pakistanis who want to stand up to violent extremism.

In a short span, we have taken significant strides to translate the promise of these technologies into results that make a difference. But there is still so much more to be done. And as we work together with the private sector and foreign governments to deploy the tools of 21st century statecraft, we have to remember our shared responsibility to safeguard the freedoms that I've talked about today. We feel strongly that principles like information freedom aren't just good policy, not just somehow connected to our national values, but they are universal and they're also good for business. . . .

Now, ultimately, this issue isn't just about information freedom; it is about what kind of world we want and what kind of world we will inhabit. It's about whether we live on a planet with one internet, one global community, and a common body of knowledge that benefits and unites us all, or a fragmented planet in which access to information and opportunity is dependent on where you live and the whims of censors.

Information freedom supports the peace and security that provides a foundation for global progress. Historically, asymmetrical access to information is one of the leading causes of interstate conflict. When we face serious disputes or dangerous incidents, it's critical that people on both sides of the problem have access to the same set of facts and opinions.

As it stands, Americans can consider information presented by foreign governments. We do not block your attempts to communicate with the people in the United States. But citizens in societies that practice censorship lack exposure to outside views. In North Korea, for example, the government has tried to completely isolate its citizens from outside opinions. This lopsided access to information increases both the likelihood of conflict and the probability that small disagreements could escalate. So I hope that responsible governments with an interest in global stability will work with us to address such imbalances. . . .

Now, we are reinvigorating the Global Internet Freedom Task Force as a forum for addressing threats to internet freedom around the world, and we are urging U.S. media companies to take a proactive role in challenging foreign governments' demands for censorship and surveillance. The private sector has a shared responsibility to help safeguard free expression. And when their business dealings threaten to undermine this freedom, they need to consider what's right, not simply what's a quick profit. . . .

Now, pursuing the freedoms I've talked about today is, I believe, the right thing to do. But I also believe it's the smart thing to do. By advancing this agenda, we align our principles, our economic goals, and our strategic priorities. We need to work toward a world in which access to networks and information brings people closer together and expands the definition of the global community. Given the magnitude of the challenges we're facing, we need people around the world to pool their knowledge and creativity to help rebuild the global economy, to protect our environment, to defeat violent extremism, and build a future in which every human being can live up to and realize his or her God-given potential. . . .

So let us recommit ourselves to this cause. Let us make these technologies a force for real progress the world over. And let us go forward together to champion these freedoms for our time, for our young people who deserve every opportunity we can give them.

The US Government Will Work with Other Nations to Establish International Internet Policies

The White House

The following viewpoint is an official report prepared by White House staff and signed by President Barack Obama.

The cyberspace environment that we seek rewards innovation and empowers individuals; it connects individuals and strengthens communities; it builds better governments and expands accountability; it safeguards fundamental freedoms and enhances personal privacy; it builds understanding, clarifies norms of behavior, and enhances national and international security. To sustain this environment, international collaboration is more than a best practice; it is a first principle.

A Cyberspace that Empowers and Endures

At the core of digital innovation is the ability to add new functionality to networked machines. The openness of digital systems explains their explosive growth, rapid development, and enduring importance. Networked technology's basic tools are steadily increasing in availability and decreasing in price, as computer and Internet access have spread to every nation. To continue to serve the needs of an ever-growing wired population, manufacturers of hardware and operating systems must continue to empower the widest possible range of developers across the globe. As companies continue to drive innovation in the development of proprietary software, we also applaud

International Strategy for Cyberspace, The White House, May 2011.

the vibrancy of the open-source software movement, giving developers and consumers the choice of community-driven solutions to meet their needs.

The United States supports an Internet with end-to-end interoperability, which allows people worldwide to connect to knowledge, ideas, and one another through technology that meets their needs. The free flow of information depends on interoperability—a principle affirmed by 174 nations in the Tunis Commitment of the World Summit on the Information Society. The alternative to global openness and interoperability is a fragmented Internet, where large swaths of the world's population would be denied access to sophisticated applications and rich content because of a few nations' political interests. The collaborative development of consensus-based international standards for information and communication technology is a key part of preserving openness and interoperability, growing our digital economies, and moving our societies forward.

For cyberspace as we know it to endure, our networked systems must retain our trust. Users need to have confidence that their data will be secure in transit and storage, as well as reliable in delivery. An effective strategy will require action on many fronts, with shared responsibility at every level of society, from the end-user up through collaboration among nation-states.

Vulnerability reduction will require robust technical standards and solutions, effective incident management, trustworthy hardware and software, and secure supply chains. Risk reduction on a global scale will require effective law enforcement; internationally agreed norms of state behavior; measures that build confidence and enhance transparency; active, informed diplomacy; and appropriate deterrence. Finally, incident response will require increased collaboration and technical information sharing with the private sector and international community. This work cannot be fully addressed by any single nation or sector alone; it is a responsibility and duty that every nation, and its people, all share.

Network stability is a cornerstone of our global prosperity, and securing those networks is more than strictly a technical matter. Economically, we must advance sustainable growth and invest in infrastructure at home and abroad, while incentivizing network reliability and clarifying the obligations of firms and states. Politically, we must help to maintain an environment of respect for technical infrastructure, so disputes do not become excuses to disrupt and degrade networks. Socially, we must make end-users aware of their responsibilities to maintain and operate their devices in a safe and secure manner.

We will continue to work internationally to forge consensus regarding how norms of behavior apply to cyberspace.

Stability Through Norms

The United States will work with like-minded states to establish an environment of expectations, or norms of behavior, that ground foreign and defense policies and guide international partnerships. The last two decades have seen the swift and unprecedented growth of the Internet as a social medium; the growing reliance of societies on networked information systems to control critical infrastructures and communications systems essential to modern life; and increasing evidence that governments are seeking to exercise traditional national power through cyberspace. These events have not been matched by clearly agreed-upon norms for acceptable state behavior in cyberspace. To bridge that gap, we will work to build a consensus on what constitutes acceptable behavior, and a partnership among those who view the functioning of these systems as essential to the national and collective interest.

The Role of Norms. In other spheres of international relations, shared understandings about acceptable behavior have enhanced stability and provided a basis for international action when corrective measures are required. Adherence to such norms brings predictability to state conduct, helping prevent the misunderstandings that could lead to conflict.

The development of norms for state conduct in cyberspace does not require a reinvention of customary international law, nor does it render existing international norms obsolete. Longstanding international norms guiding state behavior—in times of peace and conflict—also apply in cyberspace. Nonetheless, unique attributes of networked technology require additional work to clarify how these norms apply and what additional understandings might be necessary to supplement them. We will continue to work internationally to forge consensus regarding how norms of behavior apply to cyberspace, with the understanding that an important first step in such efforts is applying the broad expectations of peaceful and just interstate conduct to cyberspace.

The Basis for Norms. Rules that promote order and peace, advance basic human dignity, and promote freedom in economic competition are essential to any international environment. These principles provide a basic roadmap for how states can meet their traditional international obligations in cyberspace and, in many cases, reflect duties of states that apply regardless of context. The existing principles that should support cyberspace norms include:

- Upholding Fundamental Freedoms: States must respect fundamental freedoms of expression and association, online as well as off.

- Respect for Property: States should in their undertakings and through domestic laws respect intellectual property rights, including patents, trade secrets, trademarks, and copyrights.

- Valuing Privacy: Individuals should be protected from arbitrary or unlawful state interference with their privacy when they use the Internet.

- Protection from Crime: States must identify and prosecute cybercriminals, to ensure laws and practices deny criminals safe havens, and cooperate with international criminal investigations in a timely manner.

- Right of Self-Defense: Consistent with the United Nations Charter, states have an inherent right to self-defense that may be triggered by certain aggressive acts in cyberspace.

The United States will combine diplomacy, defense, and development to enhance prosperity, security, and openness so all can benefit from networked technology.

Deriving from these traditional principles of interstate conduct are responsibilities more specific to cyberspace, focused in particular on preserving global network functionality and improving cybersecurity. Many of these responsibilities are rooted in the technical realities of the Internet. Because the Internet's core functionality relies on systems of trust (such as the Border Gateway Protocol), states need to recognize the international implications of their technical decisions, and act with respect for one another's networks and the broader Internet. Likewise, in designing the next generation of these systems, we must advance the common interest by supporting the soundest technical standards and governance structures, rather than those that will simply enhance national prestige or political control. Emerging norms, also essential to this space, include:

- Global Interoperability: States should act within their authorities to help ensure the end-to-end interoperability of an Internet accessible to all.

- Network Stability: States should respect the free flow of information in national network configurations, ensuring they do not arbitrarily interfere with internationally interconnected infrastructure.

- Reliable Access: States should not arbitrarily deprive or disrupt individuals' access to the Internet or other networked technologies.

- Multi-stakeholder Governance: Internet governance efforts must not be limited to governments, but should include all appropriate stakeholders.

- Cybersecurity Due Diligence: States should recognize and act on their responsibility to protect information infrastructures and secure national systems from damage or misuse.

While cyberspace is a dynamic environment, international behavior in it must be grounded in the principles of responsible domestic governance, peaceful interstate conduct, and reliable network management. As these ideas develop, the United States will foster and participate fully in discussions, advancing a principled approach to Internet policy-making and developing shared understandings in fora appropriate to each issue.

To realize this future and help promulgate positive norms, the United States will combine diplomacy, defense, and development to enhance prosperity, security, and openness so all can benefit from networked technology. These three approaches are central to our efforts internationally. . . .

Diplomacy: Strengthening Partnerships

Extending the principles of peace and security to cyberspace—while preserving its benefits and character—will require strengthened partnerships and expanded initiatives. We will engage the international community in frank and urgent dialogue, to build consensus around principles of responsible behavior in cyberspace and the actions necessary, both domestically and as an international community, to build a system of cyberspace stability. . . .

The United States will continue to strengthen our network defenses and our ability to withstand and recover from disruptions and other attacks.

In the international arena in particular, states have an enduring role to play in preserving peace and stability, empowering innovation, safeguarding economic and national security interests, and protecting and promoting the individual rights of citizens. In our international relations, the United States will work to establish an environment of international expectations that anchor foreign and defense policies and strengthen our international relationships.

Bilateral and Multilateral Partnerships. We will work bilaterally with nations to build collaboration on cyberspace issues important to our governments and our peoples. Building broad international understanding about cyberspace norms of behavior must begin with clear agreement among like-minded countries. We will seek a broad community of partners in these efforts, and will include cyberspace issues in a wide range of bilateral dialogues, at all levels of government and across a wide range of our activities. We will advance common action on cyberspace's emerging challenges, while building on those enforcement tools and approaches already enjoying success. Furthermore, we will actively engage the developing world, and ensure that emerging voices on these issues are heard. . . .

Defense: Dissuading and Deterring

The United States will defend its networks, whether the threat comes from terrorists, cybercriminals, or states and their proxies. Just as importantly, we will seek to encourage good actors and dissuade and deter those who threaten peace and stability through actions in cyberspace. We will do so with overlapping policies that combine national and international network resilience with vigilance and a range of credible response options. In all our defense endeavors, we will protect civil liberties and privacy in accordance with our laws and principles.

Protecting networks of such great value requires robust defensive capabilities. The United States will continue to strengthen our network defenses and our ability to withstand and recover from disruptions and other attacks. For those more sophisticated attacks that do create damage, we will act on well-developed response plans to isolate and mitigate disruption to our machines, limiting effects on our networks, and potential cascade effects beyond them.

Strength at Home. Ensuring the resilience of our networks and information systems requires collective and concerted national action that spans the whole of government, in collaboration with the private sector and individual citizens. . . .

Strength Abroad. . . . Today, through existing and developing collaborations in the technical and military defense arenas, nations share an unprecedented ability to recognize and respond to incidents—a crucial step in denying would-be attackers the ability to do lasting damage to our national and international networks. However, a globally distributed network requires globally distributed early warning capabilities. We must continue to produce new computer security incident response capabilities globally, and to facilitate their interconnection and enhanced computer network defense. The United States has a shared interest in assisting less developed nations to build capacity for defense, and in collaboration with our partners, will intensify our focus on this area. Building relationships with friends and allies will increase collective security across the international community.

The United States will ensure that the risks associated with attacking or exploiting our networks vastly outweigh the potential benefits. We fully recognize that cyberspace activities can have effects extending beyond networks; such events may require responses in self-defense. Likewise, interconnected networks link nations more closely, so an attack on one nation's networks may have impact far beyond its borders.

The United States will respond to hostile acts in cyberspace as we would to any other threat to our country.

In the case of criminals and other non-state actors who would threaten our national and economic security, domestic deterrence requires all states have processes that permit them to investigate, apprehend, and prosecute those who intrude or disrupt networks at home or abroad. . . .

When warranted, the United States will respond to hostile acts in cyberspace as we would to any other threat to our country. All states possess an inherent right to self-defense, and we recognize that certain hostile acts conducted through cyberspace could compel actions under the commitments we have with our military treaty partners. We reserve the right to use all necessary means—diplomatic, informational, military, and economic—as appropriate and consistent with applicable international law, in order to defend our Nation, our allies, our partners, and our interests. In so doing, we will exhaust all options before military force whenever we can; will carefully weigh the costs and risks of action against the costs of inaction; and will act in a way that reflects our values and strengthens our legitimacy, seeking broad international support whenever possible.

Development: Building Prosperity and Security

The United States will continue to demonstrate our conviction that the benefits of a connected world are universal. The virtues of an open, interoperable, secure, and reliable cyberspace should be more available than they are today, and as the world's leading information economy, the United States is committed to ensuring others benefit from our technical resources and expertise.

Our Nation can and will play an active role in providing the knowledge and capacity to build and secure new and existing digital systems, and in so doing, build consensus among states to behave as responsible stakeholders. Building capacity to realize these goals is not a short-term expenditure, but a wise long-term investment and a commitment on the part of our government for continued engagement.

Prosperity cannot be built on a foundation of fear and unreliability, and the United States is committed to helping build cybersecurity capacity alongside states' own technological development.

Building technical capacity. Access to networked technology is increasingly a basic need for development. Governments and industry have made a number of meaningful steps to enhance connectivity to end-users across un-served or underserved regions. International information infrastructures continue to mature and expand, providing more nations with the opportunity to access the global flow of information. The growth of the networks worldwide, and expansion of access to them, enriches the world community, yet also presents new challenges and opportunities for collaboration on issues of traditional and cybersecurity. Much of this capacity will result from private-sector investment, and the United States will work with governments and industry to build a climate friendly to those efforts, and in which they can be leveraged to address countries' core development needs.

Governments are a major determinant of whether this new connectivity produces positive outcomes or wastes its potential. Those states that have benefitted most from our capacity-building efforts are those that embrace technology to build prosperity and enhance social cohesion, rather than restrict access for the purposes of political control. For that reason, technical projects that the United States supports will by design enhance security and commerce, safeguard the free flow of information, and promote the global interoperability of networks.

Building cybersecurity capacity. Prosperity cannot be built on a foundation of fear and unreliability, and the United States is committed to helping build cybersecurity capacity alongside states' own technological development. Enhancing national-level cybersecurity among developing nations is of immediate and long-term benefit, as more states are equipped to confront threats emanating from within their borders and in turn, build confidence in globally interconnected networks and cooperate across borders to combat criminal misuse of information technologies. It is also essential to cultivating dynamic, international research communities able to take on next-generation challenges to cybersecurity.

Acknowledging that cybersecurity is a global issue that must be addressed with national efforts on the part of all countries, we will expand and regularize initiatives focused on cybersecurity capacity building—with enhanced focus on awareness-raising, legal and technical training, and support for policy development. . . .

Building policy relationships. The United States' capacity-building assistance is envisioned as an investment, a commitment, and an important opportunity for dialogue and partnership. As countries develop a stake in cyberspace issues, we intend our dialogues to mature from capacity-building to active economic, technical, law enforcement, defense and diplomatic collaboration on issues of mutual concern. We will also facilitate relationships among countries developing cybersecurity capacity—using both regional fora and technical bodies possessing specialized expertise—and will continue to promote the sharing of best practices, lessons learned, and international technical exchanges.

The US Government Should Insist that Major Social Websites Protect Privacy

Cory Doctorow

Cory Doctorow is a science fiction author, technology activist, journalist, and blogger. He was formerly Director of European Affairs for the Electronic Frontier Foundation and now lives in London, England.

It's been a year since I reviewed *The Net Delusion*, Evgeny Morozov's skeptical take on the internet's role in global justice struggles.

Central to Morozov's critique was the undeniable fact that Facebook, Twitter, YouTube and other social media tools are monumentally unsuited to use in hostile revolutionary settings, because while they may get the word out about forthcoming demonstrations and the outrages that provoke them, they also expose their users to retribution from oppressive governments.

What's more, they reveal the social ties between dissidents, making it easy for secret policemen to swoop in and round up whole movements without having to bother with the tedious business of wiretapping and surveillance in order to figure out whom to arrest.

At the time, I argued that the risks presented by these tools weren't inherent. There's no reason that you couldn't design a Facebook-like tool that helped galvanise and organise a Tunisian resistance without exposing its users to arrest and torture (for starters, you could simply abolish Facebook's "real-name" requirement and allow users to use pseudonyms).

But given the context in which Facebook arose—a Harvard lark that became a global targeted advertising powerhouse—there's no reason that anyone involved in the system's design and upkeep would ever think to harden the system against attack by dictators and their apparatchiks.

Now that the need was visible, people who cared about the plight of those who suffer in oppressive regimes would work with those people to develop tools that helped to network their users without exposing their users.

And indeed, the last year [2011] has seen enormous energy put into this task, with extensive development of Wikileaks-style whistleblowing platforms, anonymising tools like Tor, and accessible primers on their use.

So far, so good. But last night [January 2012], I listened to Ethan Zuckerman's 2011 Vancouver Human Rights lecture, "Cute Cats and The Arab Spring," and I realised that Morozov and I were *both* wrong. Zuckerman is the director of [Massachusetts Institute of Technology] MIT's Centre for Civic Media and the founder of Geekcorps, an NGO [nongovernmental organization] that sends technologists to the developing world to work on locally initiated, sustainable technology initiatives.

He knows an awful lot of the daily, gritty reality of the internet's place in free speech and justice contexts in some of the world's most brutal and censorious regimes.

The whole speech is worth listening to, but I was especially taken by Zuckerman's "cute cats theory" of internet revolution.

The Internet Is the Best Place for Dissent to Start

Zuckerman's argument is this: while YouTube, Twitter, Facebook (and other popular social services) aren't good at protecting dissidents, they are nevertheless the best place for this sort of activity to start, for several reasons.

First, because when YouTube is taken off your nation's internet, everyone notices, not just dissidents. So if a state shuts down a site dedicated to exposing official brutality, only the people who care about that sort of thing already are likely to notice.

Revolutions are touched off by everyday people with everyday grievances . . . and those people will use the tools they are familiar with to get the word out.

But when YouTube goes dark, all the people who want to look at cute cats discover that their favourite site is gone, and they start to ask their neighbours why, and they come to learn that there exists video evidence of official brutality so heinous and awful that the government has shut out all of YouTube in case the people see it.

Second, the most common tool used by oppressive regimes against dissident sites is distributed denial of service (DDOS), sending floods of traffic from networks of thousands of compromised PCs that overwhelms the target server and knocks it off the internet.

Services such as Twitter, Facebook and YouTube are much better at surviving these attacks than a home-brewed dissident site.

Finally, Zuckerman argues that the lesson from the Arab spring is that revolutions are touched off by everyday people with everyday grievances—arbitrary detention, corruption and police brutality—and those people will use the tools they are familiar with to get the word out.

The first thing that comes to mind after you capture a mobile phone video of the police murdering a family member isn't "Let's see, I wonder if there's a purpose-built activist tool that I can use for distributing this clip?" Rather, the first thing that comes to mind is, "I'd better post this on Facebook/YouTube/Twitter so that everyone can see it."

This last argument is the most convincing to me. While activist tools are vital to a continuing struggle, they're never going to be the system of first recourse when disaster strikes.

Popular Internet Social Tools Should Protect Privacy

Which means that the only way to keep activists, dissidents, and those who struggle against brutal oppression safe is to somehow convince the people who make the world's most popular social tools to harden them from the get-go.

We have to convince our own governments that when they mandate snoopy back-doors and kill-switches in social media, they give that capacity to dictators, too.

This is an uphill task to begin with, but it is only made harder by the demands of "liberal" governments in Europe, Canada, the US and other "free" countries who want to be sure that they can spy on their own populations with social media.

Add to that legislative insanity like the pending US Stop Online Piracy Act (SOPA), which requires services to spy on their users and delete links to infringing content, and the problem becomes three times as hard.

It's not a pretty picture. And yet, at least, it gives us a road map.

First, we have to convince our own governments that when they mandate snoopy back-doors and kill-switches in social media, they give that capacity to dictators, too.

Secondly, we have to make the connection between copyright enforcement surveillance and global justice struggles, by explaining as often as necessary that you can't make a system that prevents spying by secret police and allows spying by media giants.

And finally, we have to convince these businesses that it is in their interests to make the architectural changes that protect their users from arbitrary detention, torture and murder when they make the unplanned transition from cute cats to impromptu atrocity videographer.

That's 2012, then, and several of the years that will follow. Let's get busy.

Internet Activism Has Little Impact on Promoting Democracy in Closed Societies

Evgeny Morozov

Evgeny Morozov, who was born in Belarus, is a visiting scholar at Stanford University and a contributing editor to Foreign Policy *magazine. He is well known for his book* The Net Delusion: The Dark Side of Internet Freedom, *which has been widely discussed by commentators on Internet activism.*

The only place where the West is still unabashedly eager to promote democracy is in cyberspace. Enthusiastic belief in the liberating power of technology, accompanied by the irresistible urge to enlist Silicon Valley start-ups in the global fight for freedom, is of growing appeal to many policy makers. In fact, many of them are as upbeat about the revolutionary potential of the Internet as their colleagues in the corporate sector were in the 1990s.

We shouldn't give the Internet too much credit, however, and we should probably give it credit for some of the negative things that are happening. We shouldn't be biased and just look at the brighter side. We should be more critical in thinking about its impacts.

Cyber-Utopianism and Cyber-Realism

The idea that the Internet favors the oppressed rather than the oppressor is marred by what I call cyber-utopianism: a naïve belief in the emancipatory nature of online communication that rests on a stubborn refusal to acknowledge its downside.

Cyber-utopians ambitiously set out to build a new and improved United Nations, only to end up with a digital Cirque du Soleil. Failing to anticipate how authoritarian governments would respond to the Internet, cyber-utopians did not predict how useful the Internet would prove for propaganda purposes, how masterfully dictators would use it for surveillance, and how sophisticated modern forms of Internet censorship would become.

Fidel Castro's Twitter page has been around for a few years. But very few people in Cuba own computers, because the Cuban government restricted the sale of computers to its population, so most of them just don't have the equipment to tweet. They don't have Internet cafés. They do have a small blogging culture, a few bloggers who have to be very careful. The government modified the restrictions on computers only a short while ago, so I wouldn't expect Facebook or Twitter to matter much in Cuba in the next five to ten years.

Digital activists in the Middle East can boast quite a few accomplishments . . . but I don't think the Internet will play much of a role in Middle Eastern democratic revolutions compared with other factors.

Take a closer look at the blogospheres in almost any authoritarian regime, and you are likely to discover that they are teeming with nationalism and xenophobia. Things don't look particularly bright for the kind of flawless democratization that some expect from the Internet's arrival.

Likewise, bloggers uncovering and publicizing corruption in local governments could be—and are—easily co-opted by higher-ranking politicians and made part of the anti-corruption campaign. The overall impact on the strength of the regime in this case is hard to determine; the bloggers may be diminishing the power of local authorities but boosting the power of the federal government. Authoritarian regimes in Central Asia, for example, have been actively promoting a host of e-government initiatives.

Normally a regime that fights its own corruption has more legitimacy with its own people. From that perspective, I wouldn't go so far as to say that the Internet is making the government more accountable, but I would say that it is making local officials more responsible.

The government may be eliminating corruption in the provinces, making the people happier, but that doesn't mean that they're eliminating corruption at the top. So the distribution of corruption might be changing. But I do think government might use the Internet to solicit more citizen input. That won't undermine the government. It will bolster its legitimacy.

It's not paradoxical. The fact that the government is soliciting their opinions does not mean that the government is listening to them. It wants to give the people the impression that it is listening to them. In some sense, it creates a semblance of democratic institutions. It's all about creating a veneer of legitimacy.

The Internet's Role in Middle Eastern Revolutions

Digital activists in the Middle East can boast quite a few accomplishments, particularly when it comes to documenting police brutality, but I don't think the Internet will play much of a role in Middle Eastern democratic revolutions compared with other factors. The things to watch for are how the new leaders shape the new constitutions and how they deal with the elements of the previous regimes. All those things are far more important than what happens online. I wouldn't bet that the Internet will be a great help.

As for the extent to which these new regimes become democracies—it's a wild guess for anyone, me included. They have a chance, but outcomes will depend upon many factors, including internal policies and external conflicts. I don't buy into the cultural notion of Arabs not being ready for democracy. Democracy in the Middle East may succeed. But it will depend on how they work with the existing challenges.

A regime's response to a revolt depends on the regime, not on the Internet.

The revolts were driven by people who had economic grievances and were politically oppressed. They turned to the Internet to publicize their grievances and their resistance. The fact that new media and blogs were present probably set a different tempo to the revolts. If the Internet were not around, the regime might be tempted to crack down in a much more brutal way. The revolts themselves would be taking a different shape, and they may have happened three to six months later.

It's hypothetical to say how today's democratic revolutions would have happened without the Internet, but revolutions throughout history are driven by cultural factors. The events probably would have happened differently and probably would have turned out differently. We have to entertain the possibility that these events could have been much more violent and taken much more time if they hadn't had the publicity that they had thanks to the Internet.

But ultimately, a regime's response to a revolt depends on the regime, not on the Internet. Just because people can tweet and blog doesn't stop the Libyan government from instituting a violent crackdown.

In all, it's hard to generalize based on the future of the Internet. We don't have a one-size-fits-all approach to every country. We adapt our policies for each country. That's how foreign policy works. But with the Internet, we have a tendency to generalize that this must be how it works everywhere, and that isn't the case.

How Russia Handles the Internet and Activism

While civic activism—raising money for sick children and campaigning to curb police corruption—is highly visible on the Russian Internet, it's still entertainment and social media that dominate. In this respect, Russia hardly differs from the United States or countries in western Europe. The most popular Internet searches on Russian search engines are not for "What is Democracy?" or "how to protect human rights," but for "What is love?" and "how to lose weight."

The Kremlin supports, directly or indirectly, a host of sites about politics, which are usually quick to denounce the opposition and welcome every government initiative, but increasingly branches out into apolitical entertainment. From the government's perspective, it's far better to keep young Russians away from politics altogether, having them consume funny videos on Russia's own version of YouTube, RuTube (owned by Gazprom, the country's state-owned energy behemoth), or on Russia.ru, where they might be exposed to a rare ideological message as well.

Giving everyone a blog will not by itself increase the health of modern-day democracy.

Many Russians are happy to comply, not least because of the high quality of such online distractions. The Russian authorities may be on to something here: The most effective system of Internet control is not the one that has the most sophisticated and draconian censorship, but the one that has no need for censorship whatsoever.

I don't think there is anything unique about Russia per se. It's just that the government is smarter than the Egyptian government was about how to use the Internet. The Egyptian government didn't do anything online. It didn't engage in propaganda, deploy bloggers, or launch cyberattacks. They missed the train.

I think the difference is that the people who built up the Russian Internet ended up working for the government. The Egyptian government's approach to the Internet was very shallow, and it had to pay the price, eventually.

Giving everyone a blog will not by itself increase the health of modern-day democracy; in fact the possible side effects— the disappearance of watchdogs, the end of serendipitous news discovery, the further polarization of society—may not be the price worth paying for the still unclear virtues of the blogging revolution. This does not mean, of course, that a smart set of policies—implemented by the government or private actors—won't help to address those problems.

Revolutions Require Training and Organization

The people who were instrumental in making the Egyptian revolution happen weren't new to politics. Almost all of them were part of existing political and social forces. They had had plenty of training and organization by various Western foundations and governments. I don't think the view of this as being a spontaneous revolution was true. I myself have been to several democracy workshops in Egypt. I wouldn't necessarily view these people as atomized individuals. They have been trained offline.

But of course, you wouldn't have heard as much about it. Who's paying for those workshops? It's the U.S. government and U.S. foundations. In this sense, Facebook and Twitter are much better covers, because the uprisings they enabled appeared to be spontaneous. It would be very misleading to suggest that all the connections forged by these activists are virtual. Revolution is much more about building human networks.

In 1996, when a group of high-profile digerati took to the pages of *Wired* magazine and proclaimed that the "public square of the past" was being replaced by the Internet, a technology that "enables average citizens to participate in national discourse, publish a newspaper, distribute an electronic pamphlet to the world . . . while simultaneously protecting their privacy," many historians must have giggled.

From the railways, which Karl Marx believed would dissolve India's caste system, to television, that greatest "liberator" of the masses, there has hardly appeared a technology that wasn't praised for its ability to raise the level of public debate, introduce more transparency into politics, reduce nationalism, and transport us to the mythical global village.

Technologies tend to overpromise and underdeliver, at least on their initial promises.

In virtually all cases, such high hopes were crushed by the brutal forces of politics, culture, and economics. Technologies tend to overpromise and underdeliver, at least on their initial promises.

Which of the forces unleashed by the Web will prevail in a particular social and political context is impossible to tell without first getting a thorough theoretical understanding of that context. Likewise, it is naïve to believe that such a sophisticated and multipurpose technology as the Internet could produce identical outcomes—whether good or bad—in countries as diverse as Belarus, Burma, Kazakhstan, and Tunisia. There is so much diversity across authoritarian regimes.

I wouldn't have much hope in the Internet in North Korea. First, it's a country with some of the fewest Internet connections in the world. And second, average North Koreans have been brainwashed to such an extent that you have serious psychological challenges that you can't overcome just by using blogs and Twitter. It would be much harder than for a country like Belarus, for example, where one-third of the country is online. Mobile phones might play a role in getting more information out. But it's unlikely that Facebook or Twitter will play much of a role.

Cyber-realists wouldn't search for technological solutions to problems that are political in nature.

Policy makers need to abandon both cyber-utopianism and Internet-centrism, if only for the lack of accomplishment. What would take their place? What would an alternative, more down-to-earth approach to policy making in the digital age— let's call it cyber-realism—look like?

A Cyber-Realist Approach to Policymaking

Cyber-realists would struggle to find space for the Internet in existing pillars. Instead of asking the highly general, abstract, and timeless question of "How do we think the Internet changes closed societies?," they would ask "How do we think the Internet is affecting our existing policies on country X?" Instead of operating in the realm of the Utopian and the ahistorical, impervious to the ways in which developments in domestic and foreign policies intersect, cyber-realists would be constantly searching for highly sensitive points of interaction between the two.

They wouldn't label all Internet activism as either useful or harmful. Instead, they would evaluate the desirability of promoting such activism in accordance with their existing policy objectives.

Cyber-realists wouldn't search for technological solutions to problems that are political in nature, and they wouldn't pretend that such solutions are even possible. Nor would cyber-realists search for a bullet that could destroy authoritarianism—or even the next-to-silver bullet, for the utopian dreams that such a bullet can even exist would have no place in their conception of politics.

Instead, cyber-realists would focus on optimizing their own decision-making and learning processes, hoping that the right mix of bureaucratic checks and balances, combined with the appropriate incentives structure, would identify wicked problems before they are misdiagnosed as tame ones, as well as reveal how a particular solution to an Internet problem might disrupt solutions to other, non-Internet problems.

Most important, cyber-realists would accept that the Internet is poised to produce different policy outcomes in different environments and that a policy maker's chief objective is not to produce a thorough philosophical account of the Internet's impacts on society at large, but, rather, to make the Internet an ally in achieving specific policy objectives. For them, the promotion of democracy would be too important an activity to run it out of a Silicon Valley lab.

A Trick of the Light: The Internet Has Not Brought Us Any Closer to Freedom

Bryan Appleyard

Bryan Appleyard writes for Telegraph, *and has written for many other major publications.*

In June 2009, thousands of young Iranians took to the streets to protest against the rigged election keeping Mahmoud Ahmadinejad in power. Many of them were carrying smartphones. Videos of the uprising and its brutal suppression were broadcast around the world. The death of Neda Agha-Soltan, blood streaming from her nose and mouth, became the nightmare image of tyranny for the internet generation. Surely, after such exposure, this fascist theocracy would crumble.

Cyber-utopians in the west prepared to celebrate the fall of Ahmadinejad and perhaps even of Iran's Supreme Leader, Ayatollah Khamenei. Blogs, Twitter and YouTube were the tools of revolution. "This is it. The big one," said Clay Shirky, prime booster of the better world order being ushered in by the internet.

But it was all a trick of the light. Many Iranians hated the west more than they hated their president. Even the deluge of tweeting and blogging was not what it seemed. Much of it came from outside Iran and, anyway, the regime continued to unleash the goons. Too much was at stake to be distracted by western-centred wishful thinking. It was all, writes Evgeny Morozov, "a wild fantasy".

Morozov is an apostate. Now a policy wonk in Washington, he started out as a cyber-utopian. He believed in the

"Google Doctrine", the idea that unlimited and uncensorable flows of information would spread democracy and undermine tyranny. For somebody born in Belarus in 1984 and who witnessed the relentless stripping away of democratic freedoms in his homeland, this was understandable. Tell the world, he hoped, and the world would react with proactive disgust. But, on examining the doctrine more closely, he lost his faith. This book is a passionate and heavily researched account of the case against the cyber-utopians.

Many have claimed credit for the collapse of Soviet communism in 1989, none more so than the information believers. In their account, radio, television and samizdat undermined the credibility and morale of the fumbling Russian gerontocracy. For Morozov, East Germany disproved this theory. Unlike most populations in the Soviet bloc, East Germans were exposed to the joys of capitalist life through West German television. Far from radicalising the people, it seemed to make them more compliant. This, Morozov glumly observes, is what is happening in Putin's Russia. Online, via Chatroulette—try it and be very depressed—and *The Tits Show*, the Russian people are being distracted from the onset of neo-Stalinism.

The internet is overwhelmingly used for entertainment, distraction and social networking.... [It] spawns more giggling or aroused couch potatoes than angry activists.

But the information myth persisted. It gained further traction because, for Francis Fukuyama and others, the fall of communism represented the history-ending triumph of liberal democratic capitalism. If this was the only way, surely we had only to explain that to the rest of the world and they would all fall into line. The partially televised slaughter in Tiananmen Square in 1989 made the point. "Let the people think for themselves and speak their minds ... or smell your economy rot," crowed the US magazine the *New Republic*.

The arrival of the internet for the masses in the Nineties, and especially the appearance of interactive Web 2.0 and broadband after the dotcom crash in 2000, reinforced the myth. As it became clear, after the 11 September 2001 attacks, that history was taking slightly longer to end than expected, the cyber-utopians became frenzied. Now only technology could save the world. Similar claims had been made for newspapers, radio and television. All new information technologies generated Utopian dreams, all of which proved illusory. But the internet, which seemed to be capable of circumventing all attempts at censorship, would be different.

Two seldom articulated ideological assumptions lay behind cyber-utopianism as it emerged in the Noughties. The first was that Fukuyama was right: liberal democracy was, indeed, the end of history. The second was that the internet was necessarily liberal and democratic. There was a third assumption, which was really about marketing: it was assumed that information itself was a political force.

Morozov easily disposes of all three. The third is the easiest. The internet is overwhelmingly used for entertainment, distraction and social networking. Porn and lolcats are infinitely more popular video hits than filmed evidence of Burmese atrocities or North Korean starvation. The internet spawns more giggling or aroused couch potatoes than angry activists.

Virtual resistance is not resistance until it takes to the streets and, on the whole, it doesn't.

The technological belief in the end of history is based on the faith that, confronted with the cornucopia of freedom's delights, people will want to be like western secular consumers. In fact, as Morozov shows, the net has given new life to both nationalism and cultish religions. Take the Turkish village of Gokce, where polygamy is still practised. Men from there used to travel to Syria to find wives; now they find it much easier in internet cafés.

As for internet democracy, its spread is being thwarted at every turn. The Chinese have shown amazing ingenuity in controlling the net and, less ingenious but equally effective, the Saudis disabled Tomaar, a web forum devoted to the discussion of philosophy, an idea that the Saudi authorities felt threatened the primacy of Islam. They did so by the crude means of "distributed denial of service" attacks. These swamp sites with so many hits that the ventures become too expensive to maintain and are destroyed. Western countries, meanwhile, are evolving their own forms of net tyranny. Facebook and Google now watch their users with KGB-like intensity. Their databases are worth billions and the more detailed they are, the more they suck us into giving away our identities, the more valuable they become.

Yet the net boosters are right to point our that the web makes activism easier. Millions become involved through a single click. Here Morozov wheels out a surprising witness, the great theologian and philosopher Søren Kierkegaard. He witnessed the expansion of public debate in the early 19th century with dismay. Kierkegaard thought it would destroy social cohesion and produce shallow involvement rather than deep thought. In the internet age, this becomes "slacktivism"—easy clicks that produce big numbers but very little commitment. Virtual resistance is not resistance until it takes to the streets and, on the whole, it doesn't.

One fallback position in response to all this is to argue that technology is neutral, and that it is how it is used that determines its value. Morozov also demolishes this, branding it in effect as fatuously quietist. For it is the form of the technology that determines how it is used. The evils of the internet are as much a product of its form as are the goods. Only by becoming "cyber-realists" can we hope to make humane and effective policy in response to this.

The Net Delusion is a polemic and should be read as such. It is an angry and often overwritten tumult of evidence. There are arguments against some of what Morozov says, but none, I think, that can justify the full-blooded cyber-utopian position. Human beings make human things and history is a contingent, not a deterministic, narrative. Technology will not free us of these truths, but, if we are lucky, it will make them more evident.

CHAPTER 4

How Has Internet Activism Been Used in Other Nations?

Chapter Preface

In June 2009, hundreds of thousands of people in Iran joined mass demonstrations against the reelection of authoritarian president Mahmoud Ahmadinejad, which was believed to have been fraudulent. This event was watched by the whole world through messages and videos posted on the Internet, which the Iranian government's attempt to block was only partially successful. "The immediacy of the reports was gripping," said the *Washington Times*. "Well-developed Twitter lists showed a constant stream of situation updates and links to photos and videos, all of which painted a portrait of the developing turmoil." During the following months, many news media referred to the uprising as the Twitter Revolution, and in fact the US Department of State had persuaded Twitter not to go offline for scheduled maintenance during the crisis on grounds that it was important for communication within Iran. People in the United States were given the impression that the revolt had been organized via Twitter and that it was a shining example of the impact the Internet could have on the fight for freedom everywhere.

However, social media experts later pointed out that although citizen journalists were indeed active in Iran and many people elsewhere were helping them, relatively few Iranians have access to the Internet even when it is not blocked. Most of the tweeting was between people outside Iran, who excitedly watched the demonstrations as they occurred. The impact of Twitter had been measured by the number of tweets tagged #iranelection, but most of these were in English rather than in Farsi, the Iranian language. Web activity had not been instrumental in creating the revolt.

The Internet did have a major effect on informing the world about what was happening, however, especially through the videos of violence that were posted on YouTube. Notably, an amateur clip showing the bloody death of Neda Agha-Soltan, a young woman who was shot in the street, went viral and resulted in an overwhelming reaction; thousands of Internet users replaced their profile pictures with tributes to her, such as "I am Neda." The public felt an emotional connection to the people in oppressed countries that would not have existed without social media.

Since then, a number of revolutions and protests in other countries have been termed Twitter or Facebook revolutions, such as those in Moldavia, Tunisia, and Egypt. Commentators have been sharply divided as to what extent such events are caused, rather than merely reported, by Internet activity, but most believe that the early assessment of it was greatly exaggerated. "Despite all the sweeping talk about it, Twitter isn't the maker of political revolutions, but the vanguard of a media one," wrote Blake Hounshell in *Foreign Policy* magazine. "In just a short time, it has become a real-time information stream for international-news junkies. So forget all the extravagant other claims for it. Isn't that one revolutionary enough?"

The interactive Web does give citizens of oppressive regimes far greater access to information than they previously could obtain, as well as tools for widespread communication that did not exist in the past, and although so far only a small percentage of people in these nations are online, the number will grow. However, it is often pointed out that people revolt because of their hatred of injustice and repression, not because of the technology available to them, and that they have been doing it since long before the Internet existed.

There is also growing concern about the fact that repressive governments are constantly finding ways to censor the Internet and identify dissident users that they wish to punish. Activists will counter these measures with improved technology designed to circumvent them, and there is a limit to how much restriction any nation can put on Internet use since today's economy is heavily dependent on it. Nevertheless, the conflict between advancing technologies is likely to continue in the years to come.

The Role of Facebook in the 2011 Egyptian Revolution May Have Been Overestimated

Will Heaven

Will Heaven is acting deputy comment editor for the newspaper Daily Telegraph *in the United Kingdom.*

Wael Ghonim was a new media yuppie before he became a revolutionary hero. In mid 2010, you might have found the 30-year-old Google executive by the pool at his Dubai villa, or cruising around with his friends in what he calls "great cars".

Fast-forward six months and the picture has changed radically. An exhausted Ghonim holds a microphone in Tahrir square, in his native Cairo [Egypt], shouting Arabic slogans to tens of thousands of demonstrators—he has been released by [Egyptian president] Hosni Mubarak's regime after 12 days in captivity. The next day, Ghonim sounds victorious. "*This was an internet revolution,*" he tells CNN, "*I'll call it revolution 2.0.*"

What made Wael Ghonim come home? And is he right about Egypt's revolution?

The answer to the first question begins with the brutal murder of a 28-year-old Egyptian businessman, Khaled Said, in June 2010. Purely by chance, Said acquired footage of corrupt police officers dividing up seized drugs and cash. It is thought it was delivered to him accidentally, via Bluetooth, as he sat quietly in an Alexandria internet cafe. But Said didn't delete the incriminating video—bravely, he posted it online.

The details leading up to the killing are blurry. But we know that several weeks later, two of the same policemen saw

Khaled Said walking outside the internet cafe. They took him inside, and attacked. Witnesses say his head was smashed against a marble table repeatedly, before he was dragged outside and kicked to death.

For the second time, the internet comes into play. A police report claimed he had died after swallowing a bag of marijuana. But Said's family obtained photos of his battered corpse from a morgue guard. His jaw, twisted out of shape by a policeman's boot, was enough proof of a cover-up. So in defiance of the Egyptian authorities, the photos were published online by Said's cousins. They became a shocking, viral sensation.

They even reached Wael Ghonim in Dubai—so Google's head of marketing in the Middle East and North Africa decided to act. He set up a new Facebook page to display them, calling it *"We Are All Khaled Said"*, using the moniker "ElShaheed" (the martyr) to hide his own identity. By the end of January 2011, the page had more than 350,000 followers. It was then that Ghonim invited these followers to protest against the Egyptian regime on January 25.

Facebook's Role in the Revolution

This linear narrative, or at least parts of it, has enthralled a Western audience. The story explains why Wael Ghonim came home to Egypt. But it's what happened next that's really open to question.

In short, some spectators think the linear narrative continues. That Ghonim's Facebook group inspired tens of thousands of protesters to take to the streets on the 25th, which—eventually—would lead to Mubarak's downfall. On January 30, for example, *Newsweek* asked, *"Who is ElShaheed?"* The anonymous activist, said the magazine, was *"behind Egypt's revolt"*.

Once he revealed his identity, the same magazine profiled Wael Ghonim as *"the Facebook freedom fighter"*. The *New York Times*, meanwhile, breathlessly gave an account of *"Wael Ghonim's Egypt"*—it would be Ghonim, the article said, who would "declare liberated Egypt open for business".

The protests ... would probably have occurred without the help of Facebook or other social networks like Twitter.

But other spectators—including me—aren't so sure that Ghonim organised a revolution. Or that he was behind Egypt's revolt. Or, indeed, that this was an internet revolution—"a revolution 2.0". The linear narrative has, it seems, been stretched and repackaged, but it just isn't accurate. For his part, the Google marketing executive is an undoubtedly courageous man. But he's not necessarily right.

First, let's start with the basics. What proportion of Egypt's 3.4 million Facebook users followed Wael Ghonim's "We Are All Khaled Said" page in January 2011? We haven't got a clue how many were actually in the country. At the time of writing, it was possible to follow the page using my own Facebook account in the UK. How many others followed the page from outside Egypt? How many tens of thousands of the Arab diaspora—American Egyptians, for instance? Nobody knows.

The turnout on January 25 set a historic precedent. Did Wael Ghonim's six-month old Facebook page play a part in this? Almost certainly, yes. But other factors dwarf its significance hugely, not least that Tunisia had overthrown a dictator just nine days earlier. The protests—dare one say it—would probably have occurred without the help of Facebook or other social networks like Twitter. January 25 is a national holiday in Egypt.

Then there is television. The Western media—and most Egyptians—first heard of Wael Ghonim when he appeared on Dream TV, interviewed just hours after his release from 12 days of detention. He told his story and wept for the protesters killed during his captivity. This, as one Egyptian columnist put it, gave the revolution "a shot of adrenaline in the heart". Turnout increased massively.

The chaotic reality of the Arab street protests . . . has been repackaged for a Western audience.

But this distinction is important: a significant TV interview with a social media expert—one who perhaps embodied Egypt's hopes for the future—has little to do with social media itself. The two media have been confused, and the likelihood is that television (particularly satellite television) made an enormous impact on the Egyptian revolution. As Fares Braizat, of the Qatar-based Arab Center for Research and Policy Studies, has said: "Al-Jazeera has given people a voice that they didn't have before."

The Twitter Revolution Was Exaggerated

The West has a track record when it comes to overestimating the impact of social media. Iran's Green Revolution in 2009 was known by another name—the "Twitter revolution" (among others, the *Washington Times* and the BBC World Service described it in those terms). The use of social media by the opposition movement made headlines all over the world. As Clay Shirky alleged at the time: "*This is it. The big one. This is the first revolution that has been catapulted onto a global stage and transformed by social media.*"

But the Twitter revolution was exaggerated. In Evgeny Morozov's book *The Net Delusion* he shows that, according to analysis by Sysomos (a social media analysis company), there were "only 19,235 Twitter accounts registered in Iran (0.027 percent of the population) on the eve of the 2009 elections." In other words, as Hamid Tehrani, the Persian editor of Global Voices, said a year later: "The West was focused not on the

Iranian people but on the role of Western technology. . . . Twitter was important in publicising what was happening, but its role was overemphasised."

The same is likely to be true of Egypt's revolution and the Arab uprisings more generally. The Western media has focused intently on the role of Western technology, but less so on the fact that active street protests, a strikingly familiar vehicle for revolution, brought down dictators. The chaotic reality of the Arab street protests—at one point, bizarrely, there was a camel charge in Cairo—has been repackaged for a Western audience. No doubt the 30 million Facebook users in the UK [United Kingdom], and the tens of millions who enjoyed *The Social Network* [movie about the founders of Facebook released October 1, 2010] last year, welcomed that.

So, back to that second question: was Wael Ghonim right about Egypt's revolution? Was this an internet revolution? Was this a "revolution 2.0"? No, probably not.

And when you consider one of Ghonim's other sayings— *"if you want to free a society, just give them internet access"*— the idea begins to look naïve.

Iran's 'Twitter Revolution'—Myth or Reality?

Gaurav Mishra, interviewed by Katie Combs

Gaurav Mishra is Asia director of social media at MSLGROUP, a communications and engagement network, and the cofounder of 20:20 Social, which was formerly known as 20:20 Web Tech. Katie Combs is a former associate producer and editor at Worldfocus.org.

The Iranian government has restricted all journalists working for foreign news organizations from reporting on the streets of Tehran, where thousands have been gathering to protest the country's disputed presidential election. What's been harder to control is social media tools like Twitter, where thousands of users post and share information worldwide.

Gaurav Mishra is the co-founder of social media research and analytics company 20:20 Web Tech and a 2009 Fellow at the Society for New Communications Research. He previously taught social media at Georgetown University and co-founded Vote Report India. He joined Worldfocus to discuss the role of Twitter in the aftermath of Iran's election.

Worldfocus: What role has Twitter played in the aftermath of Iran's election? Has there been a "Twitter Revolution"?

Gaurav Mishra: The story which I'm reading in the media is that of the "Twitter Revolution." And the story is that Twitter is one of the key things used to organize these protests, and the State Department is contacting Twitter to make sure it doesn't go down, and so on and so forth. That's the wrong story—it's the wrong story in Iran, it was the wrong story in

Moldova. There is no "Twitter Revolution." We haven't seen a "Twitter Revolution," and I don't think we'll ever see a "Twitter Revolution."

The revolution in Iran is not about Twitter. It's about Iranian people protesting against perceived irregularities in the election. It's a grassroots movement, and we're abusing it in many ways by calling it a Twitter Revolution. It's a big country with one of the biggest elections around the world, and clearly Mousavi supporters and Ahmadinejad supporters—all of them—have huge offline networks who are getting people to mobilize, getting support and getting people to come out and protest. We are underestimating the value of that network in a country like Iran or a country like India or China—that is a network which culturally matters. Even in the U.S., that is a network that matters. So we're really underestimating the value of that network by saying this is a "Twitter Revolution."

In countries like India or Iran, only single-digit percentages of people use Twitter. Clearly it's not an organizing tool.

On a scale of one to 10, if 10 means it is a legitimate revolution, I would say Twitter as an organizing tool is at five or six.

Twitter does play a very important role in some other areas. It has played an extremely important role in fixing the world's attention on the crisis, both in terms of getting individuals like you and me to focus on the crisis, and also in getting the attention of the international media and making sure this crisis gets the amount of coverage it deserves to get. The #cnnfail meme on Saturday, which basically asked why the protests were not on the front page of CNN—that's a very clear example that the activists know what they're doing. They're using Twitter to focus international attention on Iran, and to put this on the media's agenda.

It's very interesting—I see different stories happening. First is the story of the protest itself, and that's a very big, legitimate story in itself. Then there's the story about how Twitter and Facebook are being used to organize the protests. I think that's a fake story. It distracts from the real issue, from the real story of these protests happening in Iran, which are the biggest protests since the 1970s. And it's dangerous—we are telling them this is an organizing tool; that you can use this tool to organize protests. That's not the case, because in countries like India or Iran, only single-digit percentages of people use Twitter. Clearly it's not an organizing tool.

The mobile phone is an organizing tool and e-mail is an organizing tool, because everybody has mobile phones in these countries. And the first thing you do if you want to organize a protest is send a text message to everybody in your address book. That's how these protests are being organized in all likelihood, not via Twitter.

Worldfocus: How have traditional blogs fared in Iran compared to micro-blogging tools like Twitter?

Gaurav Mishra: We've seen that in all types of crisis situations—whether it's the terrorist attacks in Mumbai, the China earthquake, or the Moldova protests, or elections in India or Iran—in all these kinds of big events, Twitter is great at giving alerts. You're seeing a news cycle emerge where at first, stories are reported on Twitter. Then, blogs pick them up, they aggregate these stories and expand on these stories. They're the first slightly detailed sense of what's happening. And then the news organizations come in, and they write the 30-second piece on this, or do a deep story on it. And then we go into the context phase, where people add context to it and reference old stories—and this again happens both in the mainstream media and on blogs.

And finally it goes through that news cycle, and after that context and analysis happens, people start reacting to these stories, in mainstream media and blogs—and again, the reaction happens on Twitter. So if you go through the whole news cycle, what's happening is that in the alert stage, and in the conversation stage, Twitter plays a very important role. But in the stage of developing the story, giving it context, giving it analysis, blogs and mainstream media still play a very important role. Twitter very clearly doesn't have a role in developing the story, giving it context and analyzing why is it important.

Worldfocus: Why is it seemingly more difficult for the Iranian government to control Twitter compared to blogs and Facebook?

Whether it's blogs, social networking sites, news Web sites, Twitter, of course there are fairly simple ways to go around the censorship.

Gaurav Mishra: Here's the interesting thing about censorship and control. Typically how governments censor Web content is to ban specific URLs or specific IP addresses. So they would ban the Facebook IP address or the Twitter IP address or the blogger.com IP address or the wordpress.com IP address.

In countries where most of the bloggers are on blogger.com, once you've blocked blogger.com, you've basically blocked all the blogs in that country. However, people like me host blogs on our own URLs and on our own servers. Therefore, unless the government has a database of all the blogs which are self-hosted, they can't really block all blogs. You can block a blogging platform easily, but it's very difficult to block individual blogs which are self-hosted. Facebook is fairly easy to block because most people who use Facebook actually go to Facebook and use it there.

Twitter is interesting because most people who use Twitter don't actually go to the twitter.com Web site. Most people who use Twitter go to something like TweetDeck, which is a desktop application, or one of the thousands of desktop applications to use Twitter. Or they use it via text messages. So even though you can block the twitter.com Web site, you can't really block Twitter usage, because people can send and receive text messages, people can get tweets and send tweets on applications and it's very difficult to block.

On all these things, whether it's blogs, social networking sites, news Web sites, Twitter, of course there are fairly simple ways to go around the censorship. People who are technically sophisticated find it trivial to go around censorship using circumvention tools.

Worldfocus: Some Twitter users outside Iran have begun a campaign to change their profile location to Tehran, in order to shield Iranian Twitterers from government detection. Do Twitter users in Iran need this protection? And has it impeded or confused the flow of information from on the ground?

Gaurav Mishra: I think they do need this protection, because what's happening in Iran is that a lot of people are joining Twitter, because they're hearing about this. I saw some stats—a large number of people, some hundred, are joining every hour. The number of Twitter users in Iran is low, less than 10,000. Which means that when Twitter users join from Iran, it's very easy to track them. Sometimes people don't understand the complexity of this, and they reveal their location information. Then it becomes easy to profile them. I think it comes from a good place, this movement to change your Twitter location/handle to Iran to confuse Iranian authorities who might be looking to profile people.

I do think the Iranian government has more important things to do. I'm sure they have a very sophisticated database of known dissenters, and they will first go after these people. These people who are joining Twitter—they are pretty low on the list of the Iranian government in terms of cracking down on them.

I think it's overkill, but comes from a good place. Of course it harms the information flow. The only way you can make sense of the Iran feed right now, the #iranelection feed, is filtering by location. This misguided movement precludes the possibility of making any sense of what is happening now. It also precludes the possibility for academics to go back and make sense of it after it has happened. In the Moldova "Twitter Revolution," a lot of people went back and saw all the tweets related to Moldova. They found that of the 700 people who were tweeting about Moldova, only 200 people were actually from Moldova. So it becomes very difficult for people to do that kind of analysis when the location information itself is misguiding. It's harmful to do this in a way, because it breaks the validity of information and introduces more noise. But I think it comes from a good place, so I'm not criticizing the people who are trying to do this. Different people have different perspectives on what is important.

Again and again we call these things "Twitter Revolutions," and Twitter is not at the center of revolution.

Worldfocus: We've seen a lot of mainstream media sources quoting Twitter users in recent days. Are traditional media outlets embracing Twitter more so than in the past?

Gaurav Mishra: News organizations can't hope to break stories anymore, in the same way you're used to breaking stories, because you have limited bureaus outside the U.S., and there are millions of people with mobile phones out there who become accidental reporters, who just happen to be at the right place at the right time and happen to take a photo or a video or send a text message. What news organizations can do is hire people who understand these tools, who actively identify bloggers and Twitter users. The only way news organizations can catch up is by having these curators, who highlight news and the unconfirmed reports, and then who go back and try and verify these reports and add context to them, saying "This news came from somebody on Twitter, but this is what it means, and we verified it."

What's happening in Iran is nothing new. We've seen this happen before, we've seen this happen in multiple locations. We should stop calling these things "Twitter Revolutions." Again and again we call these things "Twitter Revolutions," and Twitter is not at the center of revolution.

Now, not only do citizens use [Twitter], but also political parties use it. In a country like India or Iran where most people are not on the Internet, political parties—especially the challengers, the incumbents don't use it so much. Ahmadinejad did not usually use these tools, the Republicans in the U.S. didn't really use these tools—but Democrats used it, Mousavi used it. These are great levelers that allow you to level the playing field with people in control of traditional media. I've seen this work in election campaigning, I've seen this work in protests—it's the same dynamics happening in different situations, used by different kinds of people. We should start looking at it realistically and stop being surprised every time this happens.

The Government of Pakistan Has Cracked Down on Internet Activism

Sana Saleem, interviewed by Paul Jay

Sana Saleem is the executive director of Pakistani human rights organization Bolo Bhi and a blogger at the United Kingdom newspaper The Guardian, Global Voices, *and* Dawn.com. *Paul Jay is a senior news editor at* The Real News Network.

P*aul Jay: During the last days of the regime of President [Pervez] Musharraf in Pakistan, tens of thousands of people were in the streets calling for an end to the military dictatorship. Okay, now, four or five years later, where are we in Pakistan? Has there been any change in human rights, in the level of democracy?*

Now joining us to talk about all of this is Sana Saleem. Sana is the CEO of Bolo Bhi, which means "speak up". It's a human rights organization focusing on policy and advocacy. And she blogs at The Guardian, Global Voices, *and* Dawn.com. *Thanks for joining us again, Sana.*

Sana Saleem, writer and human rights activist: Thank you. Thank you for having me.

So the issue of human rights in Pakistan is a very complicated one, and many issues. But let's start with the question of the ability to use the internet and social media, which in many countries has helped mobilize civilian resistance to dictatorship. What's the state of internet freedom in Pakistan?

Well, the authorities have always [audio incomprehensible] ever since the media crackdown. The media crackdown in 2008, during the dictatorship of Musharraf and the imposed emergency, was the prime time for social media in Pakistan, because during that time social media sort of [incompr.] started using Facebook or—Twitter was in that time—essentially, Facebook and Skype channels to mobilize protesters [incompr.] protests and everything. So during that time, the social media scene really got caught up and really got highlighted in the mainstream media. We usually say that how Egypt did it, now we did it during the dictatorship of Musharraf, because it was used very, very effectively, SMS channels and Skype and Facebook and Facebook pages, to mobilize [incompr.] There were nearly tons and thousands of students making pages and speaking to mainstream media journalists and trying to get them to do programs and, you know, putting up videos on YouTube, because people couldn't see anything that was going on in Pakistan at that time [incompr.] police brutality during protests. We've done all of that that Egypt did now during the 2008 crackdown.

If they were to charge someone for e-crime, they try them under the Terrorism Act, which sort of also risks the life of activists.

And after that, during the dictatorship, we were expecting that because we are the same people, because this is the same technology that was used to aid democracy and end dictatorship, the government would be more sort of appreciative of [incompr.] That hasn't happened. Pakistani government has since—in fact, even before Musharraf, has actively sort of cracked down on the Internet. But after the 2008 protests, especially, there's been a lot of crackdown. There's no [incompr.] no transparency in the number of sites that have been blocked. And usually these are blocked on the basis of either blasphemous content—and, again, it's very vague—or suggesting that these are against national security. So, for example, Baloch national websites were heavily blocked. Websites reporting genocide in Balochistan have been heavily blocked. There are lots and lots of—because in Balochistan there is essentially no local newspapers, or local newspapers there are not [incompr.] in the rest of the country.

And just very likely, for people that don't know the situation, Balochistan is a very, very poor and very, very resource-rich section of Pakistan that has a national struggle. And there's a lot of conflict there with the Pakistani military. Is that right?

Yes. There's a lot of conflict, and it's just sort of worsened in the recent times because of all these abductions that have happened and because these—there are a lot of—over the past two years, a lot of dead bodies and mutilated dead bodies have shown up on roadsides. And because there's absolutely no coverage, it's a media black hole, Baloch activists have actively used social media to sort of—now they're actually using Twitter as well, but they've been actively using [incompr.] to create—like, put up pictures of mutilated bodies and to report the human rights crisis.

So the Pakistan Telecommunication Authority has done a complete blackout of these Baloch websites. You cannot access them from Pakistan. That's one angle of it, that's one angle of human rights [incompr.] But they could block nearly anything without—because there's no legislation and there's no e-crime organization. So if they were to charge someone for e-crime, they try them under the Terrorism Act, which sort of also risks the life of activists who are working on this, because Terrorism Act is really hefty. E-crime is [incompr.] So they try them under Terrorism Act. Either it's that or it's blasphemy.

During 2010, we saw a Facebook blackout in Pakistan. I don't know if more people are aware, but there was a campaign called [incompr.] One of the campaign speech showed up on Facebook, and the Pakistani government decided to not only block Facebook but also deactivate all BlackBerry services. That remained blocked for months. They blocked YouTube, they blocked Google, they blocked [incompr.] and they blocked around 30,000 other websites without any notification. And it was a period of one month that was complete blackout. And it has been reinstated since then.

But what they do is the Ministry of IT or the Interior Ministry or the agencies call the ISPs and get whatever content they want blocked blocked out. It could be a Facebook page, it could be a URL. So now these telecoms and ISPs have sort of—because this blocking uses so much of their resources, they've recently, this past week, sort of opened a proposal, sent in a proposal to international companies to apply for a URL filtering and censoring system. So they'd like to acquire it. And it's going to be costing the Pakistani government around about $10 million. And in layman terms what it's going to do is it's going to allow them to block over 50 million websites, more than 50 million websites at one time. And this is—to give an example, they're going to convert the internet in Pakistan exactly—replicate the China firewall in Pakistan. So if, let's say, China does not let its citizens Google "Tibet", they could do—Pakistani government is more likely to do similar [incompr.] to Google "Balochistan" or human rights atrocities. And the deadline is on March 2, and they've already ruled out the scheme. [crosstalk]

They [the Pakistani government] can just flip—like, it's just like a switch on and 15 million websites are off, and they can add any website they want. They can do whatever they want to do with it.

And is there any indication whether Google, Yahoo!, and some of the big American companies are going to cooperate with this?

They haven't asked—. You see, that's the point. Like, they haven't asked—. With Facebook, Facebook has cooperated with them, and Yahoo! has cooperated with them. They've constantly asked Google to cooperate with them as well. They have asked big companies to cooperate with them. But [incompr.] because in Pakistan, majority of the time there's—the way the system's designed, they're not used to going to an authority and asking them to do something. They like to take control and shut it down. An example of this is a few years ago there was a video that appeared on YouTube, and it was a video of the president, President [Asif Ali] Zardari, giving a speech during a protest. And he used the word "shut up". He said "shut up" to someone in the crowd. Just to censor that video, they [incompr.] they didn't ask YouTube to remove [incompr.] and whatever. They went straight and got—in trying to get it blocked, they got the entire global YouTube system down. It was a complete YouTube blackout, global YouTube blackout for one hour because they messed the system up so much. So they've constantly not wanted any intervention from the other companies. They've just wanted to just go ahead and do it themselves.

So with this new firewall, they don't need anyone's cooperation.

They don't need anyone, yes. They don't need anyone to cooperate. They can just flip—like, it's just like a switch on and 15 million websites are off, and they can add any website they want. They can do whatever they want to do with it.

Thanks for joining us, Sana.

Thank you. Thank you for having me.

The Government of India Has Demanded Removal or Blocking of Many Websites

Simon Roughneen

Simon Roughneen is an Irish journalist currently based in southeast Asia who writes for many major publications and is a radio correspondent affiliated with Global Radio News.

The Indian government has gone on the offensive against Internet giants such as Facebook, Google and Twitter, demanding hundreds of pages be removed or blocked after political unrest erupted in various parts of the country.

On August 15 [2012], India's independence day, Indian northeasterners began fleeing Bangalore, the country's southern IT [information technology] hub and 5th largest city, after text messages said to threaten Assamese people and other northeasterners were sent around.

Authorities restricted text messages so they could be sent to only five recipients to stop bulk sending, which was followed by a government backlash against social media and news sites; more than 300 pages have been blocked in recent days.

Exodus

The scene during the exodus was reminiscent of an old newsreel from World War II Europe, or, more aptly, from the separation of India and Pakistan in the late 1940s when around 25 million people took flight amid chaos and bloodshed as the contours of the new states were drawn up after British withdrawal.

On the platform at a Bangalore train station were hundreds of people from Assam state and other areas of India's northeast, a remote part of the country almost 2,000 miles away. The region is mostly surrounded by Bangladesh, Bhutan, China and Burma and is linked to the rest of India only by a narrow strip of land nicknamed the chicken-neck.

In July [2012], fighting in the northeast's Assam state between local ethnic groups and Muslims—which some Indians say are illegal immigrants from Bangladesh—killed 80 people and forced 400,000 more from their homes, most of them Muslims. On August 11 [2012], a march in Mumbai, India's financial capital, ended up in a riot, with two killed and dozens injured, when Muslims there protested attacks on Muslims in the northeast and on Muslim Rohingya in Burma.

The SMS [short message service/text messages] scare in Bangalore came next, but who sent what and why has never been clearly established, though three men were subsequently arrested in Bangalore on suspicion of mass-forwarding threatening text messages.

Nonetheless, the scare, real or hyped, was enough to prompt panic among the 300,000 or so northeasterners who study and work in Bangalore. Interviewees at the city's rail station, waiting for a train to Guwahati in Assam state, a two-and-a-half-day journey, said they hadn't received or even seen any messages, but the rumor mill went into overdrive and their parents in the northeast urged them to come home, temporarily at least.

Apparently with public order in mind, the Indian government began blocking websites and pages said to contain inflammatory content.

A lack of confidence in police, perceived racism against northeasterners—some of whom appear east or southeast

Asian and are sometimes called "chinki" by other Indians—as well as political discord ahead of elections next year all contributed to the exodus.

Government Reacts

The Indian government urged the northeasterners to stay put, as the exodus spread to Pune, Chennai and other large cities in the south and west where northeasterners work. Text messages were limited to five recipients to stop bulk messages spreading fear, a bar later raised to 20 recipients. India has around 750 million cell phone subscribers, the world's second biggest market after China, and the government's nationwide restriction seemed an over-reaction given that the exodus was confined to a few cities.

In a country of 1.2 billion people—the world's fourth biggest economy measured in purchasing power parity terms—the government is worried about a recent economic slowdown. Growth is at its lowest since 2003, and foreign investors are complaining out loud about hazy rules and red tape. India feels it needs to nip any political unrest in the bud with foreign investment dropping by 78 percent year-on-year, according to June figures.

Apparently with public order in mind, the Indian government began blocking websites and pages said to contain inflammatory content, even as the exodus slowed.

Indian authorities blocked what they describe as "incendiary" and "hate-mongering" content on websites in Pakistan and Bangladesh that they say spurred the northeast fighting.

Nishan Shah of the Bangalore-based Centre for Internet and Society said that the government is trying to figure out how best to react to the transition from an era when news and information was carried via broadcast and print.

"In the older forms of governance, which were imagined through a broadcast model, the government was at the center of the information wheel, managing and mediating what information reached different parts of the country. In the [peer-to-peer] world, where the government no longer has that control, it is now trying different ways by which it can reinforce its authority and centrality to the information ecosystem. Which means that there is going to be a series of failures and models that don't work," Shah told PBS MediaShift in an email.

Overdoing It?

However, for a country that has long styled itself as the world's biggest democracy, and is home to some of the world's biggest selling English language newspapers, the last few days have seen the government take a forceful line against Internet giants such as Google and Facebook that some feel threatens freedom of speech.

The text messages were said to be from some of India's 170 million or so Muslim population, the world's third largest after Indonesia and Pakistan—and the Indian government at first sought to blame Pakistan for fomenting the exodus by whipping up anger among India's Muslims.

Following the text restrictions, Indian authorities blocked what they describe as "incendiary" and "hate-mongering" content on websites in Pakistan and Bangladesh that they say spurred the northeast fighting—including images of the 2010 Tibet earthquake passed off as images of Burmese Buddhists after attacking Burmese Muslims—and asked Google and Facebook to remove the content.

However, news reports on the exodus, as well as other coverage of Muslim-Buddhist clashes in Burma, were blocked. Among those affected were Doha-based news agency Al-Jazeera and the Australian Broadcasting Corporation (ABC). And stories on sectarian fighting in Arakan in western

Burma—where Buddhist Arakanese have clashed with Muslim Rohingya, with the flare-up catching the attention of Islamist groups elsewhere, including India—were blocked in India.

ABC said on Friday [August 24, 2012] content that "in relation to the particular blocked ABC, we are surprised by the action and we stand by the reporting."

An April 2011 law says that the government must give 48 hours before blocking pages, as well as an explanation for the block in each individual case, though this can be sidestepped in an emergency. "Every company, whether it's an entertainment company, or a construction company, or a social media company, has to operate within the laws of the given country," said Sachin Pilot, minister of state in the Ministry of Communications, speaking about the recent restrictions.

All told, 80 million to 100 million Indians are online, and India has the world's third biggest number of Facebook users, at 53 million. But, that just makes up just 4.5 percent of the country's population.

There's more to the back-story than just the 2011 IT law, however. Prior to the recent exodus from Bangalore and the government reaction, Google and Facebook were facing charges for allegedly hosting offensive material.

A Google spokesman, speaking by telephone from Singapore about the Indian government's recent blocks, said that the company abides by the law of the land, in India and elsewhere. "We also comply with valid legal requests from authorities wherever possible, consistent with our longstanding policy," he said.

All told, 80 million to 100 million Indians are online, and India has the world's third biggest number of Facebook users, at 53 million. But, that just makes up just 4.5 percent of the country's population.

Twitter has 16 million accounts in the country. By Friday, a stand-off between New Delhi and Twitter saw around 20 Twitter handles blocked by Indian ISPs, on the orders of the government, with threats that the government could block Twitter completely.

The hashtag #GOIblocks gets about 10–12 tweets per minute—going by a quick scroll-through—from users protesting the government's measures. However, caught up in the dragnet so far are accounts with little apparently to do with the Bangalore exodus. The Indian opposition said the blacklist is partisan, while other commentators see the government as oversensitive, using the pushback to put a block on an account (@PM0India) parodying the country's prime minister, for example.

Adding to the irony, though it is not clear whether this was by accident or design—the Twitter account of Milind Deora, the country's minister of state for communications and IT, and a vocal proponent of the recent blocks, was taken down by Twitter for 12 hours before being restored—along with an apology by Twitter on Saturday [August 25, 2012].

Internet Activism Increases in Russia

Alexander Kolyandr

Alexander Kolyandr is a senior reporter in Moscow, contributing to the Wall Street Journal *at Dow Jones Newswires.*

The recent opposition rallies in Moscow, like their counterparts in the Arab world last year, grew suddenly and unexpectedly from chatter over social networks. But they also showed the power of the Internet to raise money for anti-Kremlin causes.

Four days after an appeal went out on Facebook and other networks, organizers had raised four million rubles, about $129,000, through a Russian online-payment system. Not much by Western standards, it was a princely sum for Russia, more than enough to finance what on Dec. 24 became the country's largest antigovernment demonstration in two decades.

The money paid for a stage, a sound system, video screens and portable toilets, leaving a one-million-ruble surplus to spend on the next challenge to Prime Minister Vladimir Putin—a planned March in Moscow on Feb. 4, a month before he runs in presidential elections.

Tens of thousands of people took part in two rallies last month, angered by allegations of widespread vote fraud favoring Mr. Putin's United Russia party in parliamentary elections on Dec. 4. Opposition leaders are seeking to force the Kremlin to annul the election, stage a new vote, release political prisoners and introduce broad political changes.

Efforts to arrange a dialogue between the government and its critics have showed no progress through the New Year's holiday hiatus, which ends on Tuesday.

Mr. Putin's spokesman, Dmitry Peskov, rejected the idea of a negotiated revote, arguing that only the courts could mandate one.

As Russians celebrated Orthodox Christmas over the weekend, two powerful allies of Mr. Putin urged him to address the protesters' grievances in order to shore up confidence in his leadership.

Patriarch Kirill I, head of the Russian Orthodox Church, said in an interview on state television Saturday that the government "should adjust its course through dialogue." And former Finance Minister Alexei Kudrin, who has offered to mediate, proposed that a new parliament be elected in about 18 months under a revised electoral law. He also called on Vladimir Churov to step down as head of Russia's election commission.

For years, the Kremlin's tight control over business and civic life has made fund-raising one of the biggest challenges for the government's opponents. The task requires painstaking and delicate talks with donors fearful of official reprisals.

Alexei Navalnyi, a popular blogger and one of the leading Kremlin critics in recent weeks, raised 7 million rubles in a month last year for a website to expose corruption in government contracts.

"People are afraid of donating money openly. They are scared for their businesses, their families," said Sergei Parkhomenko, a publisher and a main organizer of both December rallies.

The Internet offered a solution. Systems such as the one operated by Yandex NV, Russia's leading search company, offer relative anonymity to donors.

Activists had used Internet fund-raising for charity and less-ambitious political projects, such as publication of anti-Putin literature.

Alexei Navalnyi, a popular blogger and one of the leading Kremlin critics in recent weeks, raised 7 million rubles in a month last year for a website to expose corruption in government contracts.

That effort drew the attention of the Russian security services, which subpoenaed the list of contributors from Yandex. Names of some contributors leaked online and donors complained of being harassed.

The first big rally after the elections, on Dec. 10, was organized in a matter of days with a modest budget covered out of the pockets of opposition leaders. As it turned out, the stage was small and the sound system far too weak to be heard by the huge crowd that showed up.

Organizers vowed to do better for the Dec. 24 rally. But the usual approaches—finding a wealthy sponsor, opening a bank account or a special-purpose company—would have been too risky or time-consuming, Mr. Parkhomenko said.

Instead, organizers turned to the Internet. More 5,000 contributions flooded in, from as little as 30 rubles, or about one dollar, to 15,000 rubles, the maximum set by Yandex. The system accepts payments only from inside Russia, rendering allegations of foreign funding moot.

"It was fast, easy and transparent. We well understood that there would be a lot of people wanting to catch us on some questionable transactions, which we have none with this system," Mr. Parkhomenko said.

Those worried that their names could be leaked made their donations in cash at the electronic-payment terminals that are ubiquitous in Russian cities.

Mr. Putin gave the funding drive an inadvertent boost when he publicly accused the demonstrators of being paid agents of the U.S. Another million rubles poured into the account within 24 hours of his comments.

"People wanted to show that not only they were not paid by anyone, but that actually they pay their own money," said Olga Romanova, the informal treasurer of the rally.

The Yandex system has a number of limitations, including caps on withdrawals, activists say. And for now, donors are more willing to contribute for specific projects, such as rallies, than for political parties.

"I hope that little by little people will stop being afraid and will start donating money openly, as it used to be" in the 1990s, Mr. Parkhomenko said.

Mr. Navalnyi said he was confident that Internet activists could contribute enough for a political party, as well.

"We raised 7 million from 20,000 people over a month," he said in a radio interview last month. "We'll raise 77,177 (million) if we need to."

Organizations to Contact

The editors have compiled the following list of organizations concerned with the issues debated in this book. The descriptions are derived from materials provided by the organizations. All have publications or information available for interested readers. The list was compiled on the date of publication of the present volume; names, addresses, phone and fax numbers, and e-mail and Internet addresses may change. Be aware that many organizations take several weeks or longer to respond to inquiries, so allow as much time as possible.

Care2 PetitionSite
275 Shoreline Dr., Suite 300, Redwood City, CA 94065
(650) 622-0860 • fax: (650) 622-0870
website: www.thepetitionsite.com

Care2 is a social action network that empowers millions of people to lead a healthy, sustainable lifestyle and support socially responsible causes. It has over sixteen million members and the petitions it hosts have generated over twenty-four million signatures in the past year. At its website, anyone can start or sign a free petition related to animal welfare, corporate accountability, education, environment and wildlife, health, human rights, media, arts and culture, politics, or spirituality and religion.

Centre for Law and Democracy
(902) 431-3688
e-mail: info@law-democracy.org
website: www.law-democracy.org

The Centre for Law and Democracy is a Canadian nonprofit organization that works to promote, protect, and develop those human rights which serve as the foundation for democracy, including the rights to freedom of expression, to vote and participate in governance, to access information, and to assemble and associate with others. Its "Human Rights and the Internet" Web page contains downloadable reports related to developing policy thinking around freedom of expression and the Internet.

Clicktivist
e-mail: contact.clicktivist@gmail.com
website: www.clicktivist.org

Clicktivist is a blog for discussing and dissecting the successes, failures, and practices of online activism. Its premise is that clicktivism is not exclusively the support or promotion of a cause online but includes the use of digital media for facilitating social change and activism by such means as organizing protests, facilitating boycotts, signing petitions, hacktivism, and online parody and satire. Its website contains short blogs on these and related topics.

Digital Activism Research Project (DARP)
website: www.digital-activism.org

DARP is producing a comprehensive database of international incidents of civic activism and nonviolent conflict in which digital media had some role in the evolution of events. Its premise is that the distinction between online and offline politics is no longer meaningful and that contemporary international relations and nonviolent conflict increasingly has causes or consequences in digital media. Its website contains an annotated bibliography of readings and media resources for the study and instruction of digital activism at the undergraduate and graduate level, as well as a few articles.

Electronic Frontier Foundation (EFF)
454 Shotwell St., San Francisco, CA 94110-1914
(415) 436-9333 • fax: (415) 436-9993
e-mail: info@eff.org
website: www.eff.org

The Electronic Frontier Foundation is the leading civil liberties organization defending the rights of the public in the digital world. It fights to defend privacy, free expression, digital consumer rights, and innovation throughout the world and educates organizations, individuals, governments, the media, and companies around the globe on the emerging threats to Internet users' rights. The EFF website contains detailed information about the activism in which it has been involved.

Fight for the Future
Center for Rights in Action, PO Box 55071 #95005
Boston, MA   02205
e-mail: team@fightforthefuture.org
website: www.fightforthefuture.org

Fight for the Future is a nonprofit organization working to expand the Internet's power for good. It creates civic campaigns that are engaging for millions of people, including the largest online protest in history: the fight against the Stop Online Piracy Act (SOPA) and the Protect-IP Act (PIPA). Alongside Internet users everywhere it beats back attempts to limit basic rights and freedoms, and empowers people to demand technology (and policy) that serves their interests. Its website contains information about its various projects.

Global Voices
Kingsfordweg 151, Amsterdam   1043GR
    The Netherlands
website: http://globalvoicesonline.org

Global Voices is a community of more than five hundred bloggers and translators around the world who work together to present reports from blogs and citizen media everywhere, with emphasis on voices that are not ordinarily heard in international mainstream media. It is an authoritative source of information about online censorship and use of online citizen media in the developing world. Its website contains articles relating to Internet activism in many languages.

Human Rights Watch
350 Fifth Ave., 34th Floor, New York, NY   10118-3299
(212) 290-4700 • fax: (212) 736-1300

e-mail: hrwpress@hrw.org
website: www.hrw.org

Human Rights Watch is a nonprofit, nongovernmental organization dedicated to defending and protecting human rights. By focusing international attention where human rights are violated, it gives voice to the oppressed and seeks to hold oppressors accountable for their crimes. Its website contains articles on dozens of topics related to these concerns, including reports on the Internet activism related to them.

Bibliography

Books

Mark Bauerlein, ed.	*The Digital Divide*. New York: Tarcher, 2011.
Jenna Burrell	*Invisible Users: Youth in the Internet Cafés of Urban Ghana*. Cambridge, MA: MIT Press, 2012.
Manuel Castells	*Networks of Outrage and Hope: Social Movements in the Internet Age*. Malden, MA: Polity, 2012.
Jennifer Earl and Katrina Kimport	*Digitally Enabled Social Change: Activism in the Internet Age*. Cambridge, MA: MIT Press, 2011.
Wael Ghonim	*Revolution 2.0: The Power of the People Is Greater Than the People in Power—A Memoir*. New York: Houghton Mifflin Harcourt, 2012.
Joss Hands	*@ Is for Activism: Dissent, Resistance and Rebellion in a Digital Culture*. New York: Pluto Press, 2011.
Tom Head	*It's Your World, So Change It: Using the Power of the Internet to Create Social Change*. Indianapolis, IN: Que, 2010.
Matthew Hindman	*The Myth of Digital Democracy*. Princeton, NJ: Princeton University Press, 2008.

Philip N. Howard   *The Digital Origins of Dictatorship and Democracy: Information Technology and Political Islam*. New York: Oxford University Press, 2010.

Mary Joyce   *Digital Activism Decoded: The New Mechanics of Change*. New York: International Debate Education Association, 2010.

Leah Lievrouw   *Alternative and Activist New Media*. Malden, MA: Polity, 2011.

Rebecca MacKinnon   *Consent of the Networked: The Worldwide Struggle for Internet Freedom*. New York: Basic Books, 2012.

Heather Mansfield   *Social Media for Social Good: A How-to Guide for Nonprofits*. New York: McGraw Hill, 2011.

Evgeny Morozov   *The Net Delusion: The Dark Side of Internet Freedom*. New York: Public Affairs, 2011.

Zizi A. Papacharissi   *A Private Sphere: Democracy in a Digital Age*. Malden, MA: Polity, 2010.

Clay Shirky   *Here Comes Everybody: The Power of Organizing Without Organizations*. New York: Penguin Press, 2008.

Sarah Sobieraj   *Soundbitten: The Perils of Media-Centered Political Activism*. New York: NYU Press, 2011.

Guobin Yang   *The Power of the Internet in China: Citizen Activism Online*. New York: Columbia University Press, 2011.

Periodicals and Internet Sources

Luke Allnutt   "Taking the Slack Out of Slacktivism," Radio Free Europe Radio Liberty, February 17, 2011. www.rferl.org.

Malaika Baxter "The Student Activist: Rebooted," *Study Magazine*, January 11, 2011. http://studymagazine.com.

Hiawatha Bray "Prometheus or Democracy?" *Boston Globe*, January 9, 2011.

David Carr   "Hashtag Activism and Its Limits," *New York Times*, March 25, 2012.

Vinton G. Cerf "Internet Access Is Not a Human Right," *New York Times*, January 4, 2012.

Alex Chitty   "Social Media and the 2011 Egyptian Revolution," May 9, 2011. http://alexchitty.wordpress.com.

Norm Cohen   "As Blogs Are Censored, It's Kittens to the Rescue," *New York Times Magazine*, June 21, 2009. www.nytimes.com.

Devin Coldewey "People, Not Things, Are the Tools of Revolution," *TechCrunch*, February 11, 2011. http://techcrunch.com.

Cathy Davidson	"Seven Reasons Why We Need Internet Activism Now," HASTAC, September 30, 2011. http://hastac .org/blogs.
Economist	"Worse Than Useless," September 16, 2010. www.economist.com.
Mark Engler	"The Limits of Internet Organizing," Dissent, October 5, 2010. http:// dissentmagazine.org.
Mike Giglio	"The Facebook Freedom Fighter," Newsweek, February 13, 2011. www.thedailybeast.com/newsweek.
Lev Grossman	"Iran Protests: Twitter, the Medium of the Movement," Time, June 17, 2009. www.time.com.
Blake Hounshell	"The Revolution Will Be Tweeted," Foreign Policy, July/August 2011. www.foreignpolicy.com.
Mathew Ingram	"Was What Happened in Tunisia a Twitter Revolution?" GigaOM, January 14, 2011. http://gigaom.com.
Dana Klisanin	"Digital Altruism: Introducing the Cyberhero Archetype," Psychology Today, July 6, 2012. www.psychology today.com.
Karen Kornbluh and Daniel J. Weitzner	"Foreign Policy of the Internet," Washington Post, July 14, 2011. www.washingtonpost.com.

Jesse Lichtenstein   "Did Twitter Make Them Do It? The Battle Over Social-Media Revolutions," *Slate*, February 2, 2011. www.slate.com.

Paul Loeb   "The Seductions of Clicking: How the Internet Can Make It Harder to Act," *Huffington Post*, July 29, 2010. www.huffingtonpost.com.

Eric Loomis   "Activism in America: Public Spaces Online and Off," *Global Comment*, August 7, 2010. http://globalcomment .com.

Evgeny Morozov   "Political Repression 2.0," *New York Times*, September 2, 2011. www.ny times.com.

Evgeny Morozov   "Freedom.gov: Why Washington's Support for Online Democracy Is the Worst Thing Ever to Happen to the Internet," *Foreign Policy*, January/ February 2011. www.foreignpolicy .com.

Evgeny Morozov   "The Great Internet Freedom Fraud: How Haystack Endangered the Iranian Dissidents It Was Supposed to Protect," *Slate*, September 26, 2010. www.slate.com.

Evgeny Morozov   "Think Again the Internet: They Told Us It Would Usher in a New Era of Freedom, Political Activism, and Perpetual Peace. They Were Wrong," *Foreign Policy*, May/June 2010. www.foreignpolicy.com.

Evgeny Morozov   "5 Reasons Why the Internet Shouldn't Get the Nobel Peace Prize," *Foreign Policy*, February 7, 2010. http://neteffect.foreignpolicy.com.

Evgeny Morozov   "The Brave New World of Slacktivism," *Foreign Policy*, May 19, 2009. http://neteffect.foreign policy.com.

Evgeny Morozov and Clay Shirky   "Digital Power and Its Discontents," *Edge*, April 12, 2010. http://edge.org.

National Public Radio   "Wael Ghonim: Creating a 'Revolution 2.0' in Egypt," February 9, 2012. www.npr.org.

Rory O'Conner   "#january25 One Year Later: Social Media & Politics 3.0," *Huffington Post*, January 25, 2012. www.huffingtonpost.com.

Jay Rosen   "The 'Twitter Can't Topple Dictators' Article," *PressThink*, February 13, 2011. http://pressthink.org.

Samantha Shapiro   "Revolution, Facebook Style," *New York Times Magazine*, January 22, 2009. www.nytimes.com.

Clay Shirky   "The Political Power of Social Media: Technology, the Public Sphere, and Political Change," *Foreign Affairs*, January/February 2011. www.foreignaffairs.com.

60 Minutes   "Wael Ghonim and Egypt's New Age Revolution," February 16, 2011. www.cbsnews.com.

Brad Stone and Noam Cohen	"Social Networks Spread Defiance Online," *New York Times*, June 15, 2009.
Berin Szoka	"Toward a Greater Understanding of Internet Activism," *Cato Unbound*, May 7, 2012. www.cato-unbound.org.
Michael Teague	"New Media and the Arab Spring," *Al Jadid Magazine*, May 8, 2011. www.aljadid.com.
Zeynep Tufekci	"Why the 'How' of Social Organizing Matters and How Gladwell's Latest Contrarian Missive Falls Short," Technosociology, February 4, 2011. http://technosociology.org.
Benjamin Wallace-Wells	"The Lonely Battle of Wael Ghonim," *New York Magazine*, January 22, 2012. http://nymag.com.
David Wolman	"Cairo Activists Use Facebook to Rattle Regime," *Wired*, July 23, 2008. www.wired.com.
Ethan Zuckerman	"Internet Freedom: Beyond Circumvention," *My Heart's in Accra*, February 22, 2010. www.ethan zuckerman.com.
Ethan Zuckerman	"The Cute Cat Theory Talk at ETech," *My Heart's in Accra*, March 8, 2008. www.ethanzuckerman.com.
Ethan Zuckerman	"The Connection Between Cute Cats and Web Censorship," *My Heart's in Accra*, July 16, 2007. www.ethan zuckerman.com.

Index